The Unread Mind

The Unread Mind

Unraveling the Mystery of Madness

Morris Rosenberg
University of Maryland

Lexington Books
An Imprint of Macmillan, Inc.
NEW YORK

Maxwell Macmillan Canada
TORONTO

Maxwell Macmillan International
NEW YORK   OXFORD   SINGAPORE   SYDNEY

This book is published as part of the Lexington Books Series on Social Issues, George Ritzer, general editor.

Library of Congress Cataloging-in-Publication Data

Rosenberg, Morris.
    The unread mind : unraveling the mystery of madness / Morris Rosenberg.
      p. cm.
    Includes bibliographical references and index.
    ISBN 0–669–27727–4 (casebound).—ISBN 0–669–27728–2 (pbk.)
    1. Psychology, Pathological—Philosophy.   2. Mental illness.
  3. Role playing.   4. Social role.   I. Title.
  RC437.5.R665   1991
  616.89′ 001—dc20   91–22729
                                                              CIP

Lexington Books
An Imprint of Macmillan, Inc.
866 Third Avenue, New York, N. Y. 10022

Macmillan, Inc. is part of the Maxwell Communication Group of Companies.

Printed in the United States of America

printing number
1 2 3 4 5 6 7 8 9 10

To Joshua Theodore Rosenberg
From a loving forbear

Contents

Preface

That mental illness is a major social, interpersonal, and psychological problem in American society today is beyond dispute. Responsible estimates indicate that in 1989 more than 36 million Americans (over 20 percent of the U.S. population) were afflicted with a clinically significant disorder. Fully 11 percent ($78 billion) of the nation's health care costs were attributable to mental illness. Despite remarkable progress in treatment in recent decades, the number of hospital admissions between 1950 and 1980 more than doubled (Manderscheid 1990). During this period the number of mental health practitioners increased nearly tenfold (Klerman 1982).

The number of persons undergoing psychiatric treatment thus seems to be approaching epidemic proportions. Furthermore, the human cost—the costs that cannot be measured in dollars—is incalculable. There is no way to quantify the amount of human suffering experienced by the mentally ill and their families or the problems caused for co-workers and others with whom they come in contact. Nor can one measure the impact on society of the widely publicized senseless assassinations and other atrocities committed by victims of mental illness.

Throughout history human beings have been both intrigued and baffled by the condition they have variously described as insanity, madness, or mental illness. This puzzlement is reflected in the different ways that the mentally ill have been viewed and treated at different historical periods and in different societies. At times, the insane have been jailed, whipped, burned at the stake, ostracized, and condemned; at other times—or even at the same time—they have also been succored, supported, protected, and cared for (Deutsch 1949; Foucault 1973). In the United States for much of the first half of this century they have tended to be cast away in enormous hospitals (appropriately called warehouses), usually in isolated areas, out of the sight and mind of most of the rest of society. Many of the homeless we see living on our city streets today continue to arouse the mixed feelings that have long characterized the American attitude toward the mentally ill: revulsion and fear on the one hand and sympathy and compassion on the other.

Why this strange and inconsistent behavior toward the mentally ill? The answer is that society has never really known what to do with the mentally ill—whether to blame and punish them or help and support them. Mental disorder has long been, and continues to be, a mysterious, puzzling, confusing phenomenon in the minds of most people.

This book is an attempt to unravel this mystery. In it I ask, What is the defining feature of mental disorder? What is it that distinguishes sanity from insanity? On what basis do human beings characterize certain kinds of thoughts, emotions, and behaviors as normal and other kinds as mentally ill?

It is remarkable how often simple questions like these are overlooked by specialists in the field. For seventeen years I held the position of Research Sociologist in the National Institute of Mental Health. At the Institute, all of the relevant mental health specialties—psychiatry, neurology, psychology, sociology, biochemistry, genetics, biostatistics—were well represented. I was thus surrounded daily by people whose professional lives were devoted to understanding and treating mental illness. Yet in all that time I cannot recall a single instance in which anyone ever raised the question, What *is* mental illness?

This work attempts to answer this question. The sociological theory I present is radically different from the psychiatric and psychological theories to which most people in the field subscribe. It is also different from other sociological theories. In contrast to those who locate mental illness exclusively within the individual, I argue that mental illness is rooted in the process of social interaction. Mental illness represents a radical rupture of the bond connecting human beings to one another. It takes two to make a psychotic—an actor and an observer. The key to the mystery of insanity, I shall contend, is the phenomenon of role-taking failure.

Acknowledgments

I owe a large debt of gratitude to the following friends and colleagues who were kind enough to review various drafts of this work and to provide me with helpful comments and criticisms: Edward Z. Dager, Jerald Hage, Lee V. Hamilton, John P. Hewitt, Carmi Schooler, and Peggy Thoits. Also, George Ritzer, Editor of the Lexington Book Series on Social Issues, made valuable suggestions which had an important impact on the final product. I am grateful to my wife, Florence R. Rosenberg, for her perceptive suggestions and advice, and to my son, Dr. Paul B. Rosenberg, who provided me with the benefit of his psychiatric expertise. Needless to say, I bear full responsibility for the defects of this work.

The author and publishers are grateful to the following publishers for permission to reproduce copyrighted material in this book.

American Psychiatric Association, for permission to reproduce selections from *Diagnostic and Statistical Manual of Mental Disorders. Third Editon-Revised.* Copyright © 1987 by the American Psychiatric Association.

University of California Press, for permission to reproduce selections from *The Meaning of Criminal Insanity* by Herbert Fingarette. Copyright © 1972 by the Regents of The University of California.

John Wiley and Sons, Inc., for permission to reproduce selections from *The Development of Role-Taking and Communication Skills in Children* by John H. Flavell in collaboration with Patricia T. Botkin, Charles L. Fry, Jr., John W. Wright, and Paul E. Jarvis. Copyright © 1968 by John Wiley and Sons, Inc. Reprinted by permission of John Wiley and Sons, Inc.

International Universities Press, Inc. for selections from *Dementia Praecox or the Group of Schizophrenias,* by Eugen Bleuler. Translated by Joseph Zinkin. Copyright © 1950 by International Universities Press, Inc.

1
Conceptions of Mental Disorder

It is a remarkable fact that after more than two millennia Western civilization has still not answered the question, What is mental disorder? Indeed, I would venture to say that the amount of disagreement has never been greater. There are well over a dozen different views, both popular and professional, that lay claim to representing the defining feature of mental disorder. In this book I will consider these competing conceptions and then advance a different view—the conception of mental disorder as role-taking failure.

In saying that people disagree about what mental disorder is, I am not referring to disagreement about its *causes*. These causal conceptions are also enormously varied. One can readily find proponents of genetic (Gottesman and Shields 1972; Rosenthal 1971), biochemical (Kety 1975), social structural (Dohrenwend and Dohrenwend 1969; Kohn 1974; Mischler and Scotch 1970), interpersonal (Mischler and Waxler 1970), interactional (Kohn 1972), socially stressful (Mirowsky and Ross 1989; Langer and Michael 1963), and other explanations. The fact that there are so many different causal explanations of mental illness does not necessarily distinguish it from many other ailments; that would be true of cancer and heart disease as well. What is noteworthy about mental illness is the fact that there are so many different ideas about what it *is*. Before discussing these conceptions I will describe more carefully the phenomenon we are dealing with.

Insanity

In the English language one finds an abundance of terms that in one way or another refer to the concept of the unsound mind. Among these are *crazy, mad, insane, deranged, demented, unhinged, mentally ill, cracked, touched, barmy, off one's head, loco, mad as a hatter, screw loose, bats in the belfry, lunatic, psychotic, madman,* and *mental case.* Such an extensive vocabulary obviously reflects a high level of awareness and rich elaboration of the concept of derangement in our society.

However varied their connotations may be, all these terms appear to share a common core of meaning. Although we easily recognize this common core, it is difficult to find a single term that will express mental disor-

1

der accurately and is at the same time free of misleading connotations. When we consult a dictionary (Random House 1966) we find that the term that appears to be most consistently cited as synonymous with these others is *insane* and *insanity*. For example,

lunatic: "an insane person"

deranged: "insane"

mad: "mentally disturbed or deranged; insane; demented"

crazy: "mentally deranged; demented; insane"

psychosis: "synonym. insanity"

mental disease: "any of the various forms of insanity"

nutty: "slang. insane"

The words *insane* and *insanity* thus capture some feature that these diverse terms have in common. Unfortunately, they also have their drawbacks. One is that they have both a technical and a popular meaning. The technical meaning is a legal one. A person is "legally insane" when judged to be of such unsound mind that he or she is excused from criminal or civil responsibility, or is incapable of entering into legal transactions. The other, more popular, meaning is reflected in dictionary definitions: "not of sound mind"; "mentally deranged"; "utterly senseless." It is this latter popular meaning that reflects the common core of meaning in these diverse terms. In this book I use the words *insane* and *insanity* in the popular sense.

As indicated above, the dictionary identifies "insanity" as a synonym for "psychosis." Contemporary psychiatry does not share that view. In psychiatry, psychosis is defined as a mental disorder characterized by a severe break with reality and is manifested in such symptoms as delusions or hallucinations, incoherent speech, and related types of behavior. Yet when one looks at discussions of insanity (other than legal ones), one finds that most of the examples represent symptoms of psychotic behavior. It is probably for this reason that, in some discussions, the terms *insanity* and *psychosis* are used interchangeably. For example, a book written by two psychiatrists (Priest and Steinert 1978) is entitled *Insanity: A Study of Major Psychiatric Disorders*. These major psychiatric disorders are primarily psychoses. When I describe the phenomenon of insanity in this work, most of my examples will also be drawn from psychosis. For this reason, I will consider "psychotic" to be essentially equivalent to "insane," that is, "not of sound mind," "mentally deranged," or "utterly senseless."

It is apparent that these terms refer to the more serious types of mental disorders. These do not, of course, exhaust the range of mental problems. There are many others that, although generally considered less serious, may nevertheless warrant professional care (although almost never hospitalization). One set of mental disorders are the *personality disorders,* such as the narcissistic, histrionic, borderline, avoidant, and passive–aggressive types. A second set of disorders are those that, prior to the eighties, were called the "neuroses". Such disorders are usually judged to be less serious because reality testing is largely intact, social norms are not seriously violated, victims recognize that their symptoms are unacceptable, and there is no demonstrable organic cause (American Psychiatric Association 1980, p. 10).

Personality and neurotic disorders often fall under the rubric of mental disorder but are almost never characterized as insanity, psychosis, madness, derangement, or any other term that refers to more serious psychological problems. It is the more serious symptoms which in the popular consciousness are associated with such terms as *psychosis* and *insanity* that I refer to in speaking of "mental illness."

Since the prototype of the functional psychoses is schizophrenia, most of my examples will be drawn from this disorder. These examples are drawn primarily from three sources:

1. Eugen Bleuler's *Dementia Praecox, or the Group of Schizophrenias* (1911/1950), a classic work on the subject. Although some of the symptoms that Bleuler described appear less frequently in clinical practice today, they nevertheless provide such vivid descriptions of schizophrenic symptomatology that they are retained for illustrative purposes. (The initials EB will be used in citations to this work.)

2. The American Psychiatric Association's *Diagnostic and Statistical Manual of Mental Disorders, Third Edition–Revised* (DSM–III–R) (1987). This work is currently recognized as the most authoritative diagnostic manual in the field of psychiatry. (The abbreviation DSM will be used in citations to this publication.)

3. The *DSM–III–R Casebook* (Spitzer et al. 1989). This work includes hundreds of cases of mental disorders that are classified according to the DSM–III–R criteria. (The abbreviation CB will be used in citations to this volume.)

Disordered Persons or Disordered Symptoms?

Before turning to the different conceptions of mental illness that appear in the literature, it is first necessary to distinguish between disordered *persons* and disordered *symptoms.* Although we usually think of the person as sick, it is actually the symptom that is disordered. This view is stressed in the most advanced diagnostic thinking. According to the authoritative DSM–III–R (p. xxiii):

> A common misconception is that a classification of mental disorders classi-
> fies people, when actually what are being classified are disorders that
> people have. For this reason, the text of DSM–III–R . . . avoids the use
> of such expressions as "a schizophrenic" or "an alcoholic," and instead
> uses the more accurate, but admittedly more cumbersome "a person with
> Schizophrenia" or "a person with Alcohol Dependence."

That we tend to think in terms of insane persons rather than insane
thoughts, emotions, and behaviors is understandable. The first reason lies
in our tendency to label people (Lemert 1972; Schur 1971). Just as a person
who has committed one or a few illegal acts and many legal ones is called
a criminal, so a person who performs one or a few insane acts and many
sane ones may be called a psychotic. Even a single prominent symptom may
suffice to identify an individual as schizophrenic (Rosenhan 1973).

The second reason is that in dealing with mental disorder we must deal
with the total person. Just as in dealing with lawbreakers we are not able
to incarcerate the criminal part of an individual and allow the law-abiding
portion to go free, so too we cannot hospitalize just the insane part of an
individual and exclude the sane portion. We therefore call a person a criminal who has committed a crime, and call a person a psychotic who has
manifested insane thoughts, emotions, or behaviors. (I follow the practice
of using the term *behaviors* to refer to a number of specific acts.)

Psychosis, then, does not reside in the person but in the symptom. In
seeking to understand the phenomenon of mental illness, we shall not ask
why a *person* is considered insane but why certain *thoughts, emotions, and
behaviors* are considered to be insane.

Consider first the question of disordered *thoughts*. Schizophrenics may
think that people are placing thoughts into their heads or removing
thoughts from their heads; that people have placed secret cameras in their
apartments in order to spy on them; that machines are placing erotic dreams
in their heads; that they have special occult powers; that all doctors are
devils; and so on (EB; CB).

Emotions may also be disturbed among the mentally ill. The schizophrenic may smile happily at a funeral; display sadness at good news; go
into a towering rage with little or no provocation; or show no emotion in
the face of exciting events.

Finally, certain *behaviors* may also be symptomatic of schizophrenia.
A schizophrenic sits in an apartment staring blankly at the walls for hours
or even days on end; displays physical rigidity or waxy flexibility; goes to
a shoe store many miles away from home to ensure that his shoes have not
been "altered"; and so on (EB; CB).

The question, then, is not why a certain *person* is considered schizophrenic but why certain thoughts, emotions, and behaviors are considered
schizophrenic. In other words, what is the *defining feature* of mental disorder?

What is meant by "defining feature"? A defining feature is one that identifies the essential quality of something. Operationally, one characteristic of a defining feature is that it is present in the presence of mental illness and absent in its absence.

In order to identify the defining feature, one must address the following question: What is it about the thought, emotion, or behavior that causes us to consider it "insane"? Consider someone who walks around with a silly grin on his or her face all the time or stares blankly at the walls for hours on end. Why do we consider such behavior symptomatic of mental illness? Why don't we consider it to be crime instead? or immorality? or bad manners? or simply an idiosyncracy or peculiarity of the individual (Scheff 1966, 1974, 1984)? Is it because such behavior is unusual? Is it because it is odd or peculiar? Is it because it is abnormal? Is it because it is socially inappropriate? Or is it because "insane" is the label we happen to have assigned to it in our society (Scheff 1966)? In other words, what is it about such behavior that undergirds our decision to characterize it as psychosis?

This work represents an effort to identify what it is about certain thoughts, emotions, and behaviors that leads us to consider them symptomatic of insanity. (In order to simplify the discussion, I will henceforth refer to these thoughts, emotions, and behaviors collectively as TEBs.) The answer to this question, I shall argue, is social, not biological.

As one explores the popular and scholarly literature on mental disorder, one cannot fail to be struck by the number and variety of different views on the subject. This fact in itself is an indication of the confusion and ambiguity which surrounds mental illness. Some conceptions are widely shared by the public, others are held only by small bands of professionals. There is no hard and fast line to separate the popular from the scholarly views. For reasons that will become clear later, it is important to give careful attention to the views of the lay public as well as to those of the knowledgeable professional.

I have classified these conceptions of mental disorder into the following categories: (1) popular conceptions, (2) psychological conceptions, (3) psychosocial conceptions, (4) medical conceptions, (5) legal conceptions, (6) interactional conceptions, and (7) societal reaction conceptions.

Popular Conceptions

Since World War II there have been a number of studies done on public attitudes toward mental illness (Halpert 1970; Rabkin 1974). They have found that in the public mind two prominent characteristics of mental disorder are *unpredictability* and *dangerousness* (Nunnally 1961; Bord 1971). According to Nunnally (1961, p. 233):

One of the cornerstones of public attitudes is the feeling that the mentally ill are highly unpredictable. The mentally ill are thought to be people who do not go by the "rules" and who, because of their erratic behavior, may suddenly embarrass or endanger others. The feeling is like that of sitting next to a temperamental explosive which may detonate without warning.

A study conducted by the National Opinion Research Center (Halpert 1970, p. 493) also shows that the general public tends to think of the mentally disordered as dangerous and unpredictable. Can unpredictability and dangerousness, then, serve as defining features of mental illness?

Unpredictability

The view that the mentally ill are unpredictable is not without foundation. According to Bleuler:

> Negativistic patients, who refuse to answer questions put to them, will at times respond to questions which are asked of others. Thus, for example, they will give the name of their own husband when one of their neighbors is supposed to answer that question. . . . The patients will withdraw their hands when they are greeted only to thrust their hand forward suddenly after one has turned to shake hands with another patient. . . . In the same fashion, they answer or wish to speak only when one is about to leave the room. (EB, pp. 182–83, 193–94)

Unpredictability may characterize the conversational patterns of psychotics. While carrying on a normal conversation, a patient may suddenly stop in the middle of a sentence; when he resumes, he talks about an entirely different topic. It is no wonder that people develop an image of psychotics as "unpredictable".

But unpredictability in itself is not a defining feature of mental disorder. Some psychotics are extremely predictable. A patient may go around with a silly grin on his or her face day after day, week after week, without the slightest change of expression. Another may remain mute for months or even years on end. Bleuler (p. 47) reports that "I observed a catatonic for ten years who . . . hurled insults at me and sat with her tongue protruding from the corner of her mouth, in a demonstrably negativistic attitude. . . ." It is clear that psychotic behavior can sometimes be incredibly predictable.

Conversely, behavior may be unpredictable without being disordered. Life is full of surprises. Teams use trick plays; drivers make sudden lane shifts; chess masters make unexpected moves; good students fail easy tests. If psychotic behavior can be predictable, and normal (i.e., sane or healthy) behavior unpredictable, then unpredictability obviously cannot serve as the defining feature of mental disorder.

Dangerousness

The popular conception of the mentally disordered as violent and dangerous is no doubt fostered by dramatic reports in the popular press of psychotics randomly shooting at strangers and otherwise wreaking havoc on innocent victims. Movies and television programs often portray psychotic killers cunningly stalking their terrified victims. Halpert's (1970, p. 494) review of studies of public attitudes toward mental illness finds that "people reserve the term 'mental illness' for behavior that frightens or antagonizes them."

This view of the mentally ill as dangerous is not new; it long predates the advent of the modern mass media. In medieval Europe psychotics were often placed behind bars, chained to walls, or subjected to other physical restraints because they were believed to be violent and out of control. Even today the involuntary incarceration of mental patients is largely based on the supposition that they are dangerous to others, to themselves, or to property (Cockerham 1989).

Although it is true that psychotics are sometimes dangerous, dangerousness is by no means characteristic of the mentally ill. Research conducted before the mid-sixties found that discharged mental patients actually had lower arrest rates than the general population (Cockerham 1989, p. 307). Although later studies showed that male ex-patients did have somewhat higher rates for rape and robbery and that females had higher rates for aggravated assault, these rates are nevertheless lower than those of ex-convicts and even of drunk drivers (Cockerham 1989, pp. 296–311). It is clear that the overwhelming majority of mentally ill persons are no more dangerous than members of other groups.

Furthermore, there is nothing dangerous about most psychiatric symptoms. What harm does a man do to others when he hears voices, stares at the wall, or feels deeply dejected? It is in fact extremely rare for psychotic symptoms to pose a threat of physical injury to anyone.

Just as mentally ill people are not necessarily dangerous, dangerous people are not necessarily mentally ill. If one defines "dangerousness" as the likelihood of inflicting harm on others, then criminals, gang members, muggers, drunk drivers, asbestos manufacturers, police officers, soldiers, and arms manufacturers are decidedly more dangerous. Since most mentally ill persons are not dangerous and most dangerous people are not mentally ill, dangerousness is clearly not the defining feature of mental disorder.

Psychological Conceptions

Psychology is a fertile breeding ground for conceptions of mental disorder. Psychological conceptions are those theories in which the defining feature of the mental disorder is located in the mental or emotional events of people or in the behavioral consequences of these internal events. I would like to consider three of these conceptions: (1) abnormality, (2) psychological distress, and (3) irrationality.

Abnormality

The view of mental disorder as abnormality represents a well-established tradition in the field of psychology. The American Psychological Association publishes a journal entitled the *Journal of Abnormal Psychology*. Numerous textbooks on mental disorder include the term *abnormal psychology* in their titles (e.g., Gallatin 1982). Among psychologists, the terms *mental disorder* and *abnormal psychology* are often used more or less interchangeably.

The term "abnormality," however, has at least three distinctly different meanings. One refers to *statistical* abnormality; a TEB (thought, emotion, or behavior) is viewed as abnormal if it is rare, unusual, or atypical. The second refers to *normative* abnormality, or deviation from socially appropriate thoughts, emotions, or behaviors; a TEB is abnormal if it violates social rules or practices. A third use of the term refers to a TEB that is *strange, odd,* or *peculiar*. Because these types of abnormality may in fact have little to do with one another, I will consider them separately.

Statistical Abnormality. That some thoughts, emotions, and behaviors of the mentally disordered are statistically rare is beyond dispute. A patient may fail to utter a word for weeks or months on end. Another, informed of good tidings, begins weeping. A third washes her hands twenty times a day. A fourth checks to be sure that the oven is off a dozen times before leaving the house. These behaviors are extremely rare.

But so are some normal behaviors. The fact that comparatively few people engage in skydiving, oboeplaying, or stamp collecting does not call into question their sanity. Artists, geniuses, jugglers, and potters all exhibit statistically rare behavior without being considered mentally disordered.

The same is true of rare thoughts. Today it is statistically rare in the United States to believe in communism, existentialism, phenomenology, or Buddhism, but no one considers such thoughts to be mentally disordered. In fact, some extremely healthy TEBs, that is, those characteristic of positive mental health, may also be extremely rare. The emotional states that Maslow (1971) identified as "peak experiences" or "oceanic feelings," although by definition unusual, are considered by many to reflect superior mental health. The fact that TEBs are statistically unusual, then, is not in itself an indication that they are mentally disordered. Statistical abnormality cannot serve as the defining feature of mental disorder.

Normative Abnormality. When most people describe certain thoughts, emotions, and behaviors as "abnormal" they are more likely to have normative than statistical criteria in mind. Normative abnormality, then, refers to TEBs that are viewed as "socially inappropriate," "wrong," or "improper."

The mentally ill often do violate certain behavioral norms. Most of the sexual disorders, for example, involve norm violations. A man may dress as a woman, expose his genitals in public, peep into windows at women, or engage in other types of behavior that offend social rules. Similarly, kleptomania, pyromania, and antisocial personality behavior all run counter to social norms. However, norm violation in itself does not indicate mental disorder. Many sane TEBs also involve normative abnormality. The robber, the pimp, the prostitute, and the speeding driver violate social norms, but their sanity is not in question.

Furthermore, what makes TEBs appear mentally disordered has little or nothing to do with social inappropriateness. The problem with hearing voices, seeing visions, or having persecutory delusions is not that they are socially inappropriate. There are no social rules stipulating that one should *not* hear voices, see visions, or suffer delusions. Whatever the problem is, it is certainly not that these symptoms violate social norms.

Thoughts, emotions, and behaviors are socially inappropriate for many reasons. For example, inappropriate behavior may be due to inadequate socialization or defective role learning. Consider the parvenu who elicits not acceptance but amused condescension from the old families. Socially inappropriate behavior may also be an act of defiance toward established authority. This was the intention of many young men who wore long hair and untrimmed beards in the sixties. Inappropriate behavior may also occur because of situational misinterpretation; for example, a man asks a woman for a date without knowing that she is married. Another source of inappropriate behavior is the loss of self-control; for example, a drunk suddenly punches a companion in the nose.

It is thus evident that inappropriate TEBs can stem from many sources other than mental disorder. As Thomas Szasz (1987, pp. 64–65) has remarked, "Jesus, Luther, the Founding Fathers, Lenin, Hitler, and Martin Luther King, to mention only a few historical figures, have all violated social norms and engaged in unconventional behavior."

Strangeness or Oddity. The dictionary provides a number of synonyms for the term *abnormality: anomalous, aberrant, irregular, deviant, unnatural, odd.* These terms often seem to apply to mentally disordered thoughts, emotions, and behaviors. Consider Bleuler's description of schizophrenic behavior:

> The intonation of the patient's speech is often peculiar. In particular, there is often an absence, exaggeration or misplacement of modulation. Speech may be abnormally loud, abnormally soft, too rapid, too slow. Thus one patient speaks in a falsetto voice, another mumbles, a third grunts. . . .

The patients may say cheerful things in a sorrowful tone, and vice versa. (EB, pp. 148–49)

In eating the spoon is held by its handle tip only or reversed. The food is taken up on the fork and dropped back again seven times before it is taken into the mouth. The patient circles the toilet bowl three times before sitting down on it. (EB, p. 191)

Such behavior certainly strikes us as strange. But strangeness cannot serve as the defining feature of mental disorder. The dress and antics of a clown are strange, but they are sane. In the past, college fraternity members swallowed huge amounts of goldfish, and in the thirties much publicity attended the achievements of flagpole sitters. There are people who choose to go over Niagara Falls in a barrel.

It is no exaggeration to say that the peculiarity of some sane people's behavior can put to shame the most regressed psychotic. Conversely, a psychopathic personality may appear to be the most normal of human beings yet still suffer from severe mental disorder. If odd behavior is not necessarily mentally disordered, and disordered behavior is not necessarily odd, then strangeness or oddity cannot represent the defining feature of mental disorder.

Psychological Distress

As noted earlier, the most authoritative work on the nature of mental disorder is the DSM–III–R. This work, published in 1987, is a synthesis of the collective wisdom, insight, and experience of hundreds of the most eminent practicing and research psychiatrists in the United States. It is in this work, then, that we find the current "official" view of American psychiatry on the nature of mental disorder:

In DSM–III–R each of the mental disorders is conceptualized as a clinically significant behavioral or psychological syndrome or pattern that occurs in a person and that is associated with present distress (a painful symptom) or disability (impairment in one or more important areas of functioning) or with a significantly increased risk of suffering death, pain, disability, or an important loss of freedom. . . . Whatever its original cause, it must currently be considered a manifestation of a behavioral, psychological, or biological dysfunction in the person. (DSM, p. xxii)

Two major characteristics of mental disorder, then, are psychological distress and social disability. "Distress" refers to pain, discomfort, unhappiness, fear, and other dysphoric emotional experiences. "Disability" refers to the inability to engage in one's normal social activities or to play one's usual social roles.

Consider first the question of psychological distress. That mental illness can be an intensely painful experience is undeniable. The sorrow, sadness, emptiness, or misery of the depressive are surely among the most painful experiences that human beings can undergo. Similarly, the phobic's terror of heights or of closed spaces may be more agonizing than the most excruciating torture. It is thus not surprising that DSM–III–R should consider psychological distress to be a key component of mental disorder.

Nevertheless, psychological distress cannot serve as the defining feature of mental disorder. The reason is that not all mental disorder entails psychological distress, and not all psychological distress reflects mental disorder.

For example, feelings of depression, though psychologically distressing, are not necessarily symptomatic of mental disorder. If someone is depressed due to the loss of a loved one, the failure of a business venture, or the experience of unrequited love, such feelings can be extremely painful, but they are not symptomatic of mental illness. The same is true of anxiety. If a soldier going into battle experiences strong feelings of fear; if a mother undergoes acute anxiety at the illness of a child; if a hotel guest experiences terror when trapped in a burning building—these emotions are as acutely painful as any that human beings can endure, but they are entirely normal. Indeed, the *failure* to experience such emotions might call into question the individual's sanity.

Conversely, mentally disordered people are not always or necessarily miserable. The good-natured hebephrenic with a big smile on his or her face shows little evidence of suffering. The bipolar patient experiencing a manic episode may be the epitome of happiness. A vivid example is provided by Clifford Beers (1910, pp. 84–85) in his famous autobiography, *A Mind That Found Itself.* He wrote:

> My fellow-patients who for fourteen months had seen me walk about in silence—a silence so profound and inexorable that I would seldom heed their friendly salutations—were naturally surprised to see me in my new mood of unrestrained loquacity and irrepressible good humor. . . . For several weeks I believe I did not sleep more than two or three hours of the twenty-four, each day. Such was my state of elation, however, that all signs of fatigue were entirely absent; and the sustained and abnormal mental and physical activity, in which I then indulged, has left on my memory no other than a series of very pleasant impressions. Though based on fancy the delights of madness are real. Few, if any, sane persons would care to test the matter at so great a price; but those familiar with "The Letters of Charles Lamb" must know that Lamb himself, at one time during his early manhood, underwent treatment for mental disease. In a letter to Coleridge . . . he says: "At some future time I will amuse you with an account, as full as my memory will permit, of the strange turns my frenzy took. I look back upon it at times with a gloomy kind of envy; for, while it lasted, I had many, many hours of pure happiness. Dream not, Coleridge, of having

tasted all the grandeur and wildness of Fancy till you have gone mad! All now seems to me vapid, comparatively so!"

In sum, if mental illness can be characterized by such surpassing joy and mental health by such profound misery, then psychological distress cannot represent the defining feature of mental disorder.

Irrationality

To many people irrationality is the hallmark of mental disorder. The dictionary, for example, defines insanity as "utterly senseless and irrational behavior." To Webster, an irrational person is someone who is deprived of reason and sound judgment or who is "utterly illogical." Fingarette (1972) contends that rationality is the critical feature of the legal definition of mental disorder. Legally a person is judged to be insane who is of such unsound mind that he or she is excused from criminal or civil responsibility, or is incapable of entering into legal transactions.

In Fingarette's view (1972, pp. 175–76), rationality is the defining feature of mental disorder. He says:

> We say of a person who is insane that he is irrational. When he manifests his insanity in his conduct, it is natural to speak of his conduct as irrational. An insane person has "lost his reason." Hadfield [a man who attempted to assassinate King George III] was a man who wished to be put to death . . . in order to play his God-ordained role as the new Christ. He was an irrational man. His attempt to assassinate the king was well thought out, but it was an irrational act.

But what is irrationality? How can one decide whether a person is irrational or has lost his or her reason? It is difficult to discover any universally accepted criteria of irrationality.

When writers speak of irrationality, I believe that they are usually referring to one of the following ideas: (1) the divorce from reality; (2) the loose connection between means and ends; (3) the inconsistency of cognitive elements; and (4) the presence of emotionally excessive responses.

Divorce from Reality. One widely recognized sign of irrationality is the divorce from reality. According to DSM–III–R (p. 404), *psychotic* is a term indicating "gross impairment in reality testing and the creation of a new reality. . . . When a person is psychotic, he or she incorrectly evaluates the accuracy of his of her perceptions and thoughts and makes incorrect inferences about external reality, even in the face of contrary evidence." Webster's dictionary identifies "defective or lost contact with reality" as the distinguishing feature of psychosis.

That the mentally disordered may be out of contact with reality is apparent. A man may think that he is Napoleon or Alexander the Great; that people in the street are whispering about him; that the woman who turned him down for a date was not the woman he asked but a look-alike; that when people snort and sneeze as he enters a room they are doing so in order to make fun of him (CB). And so on.

Yet divorce from reality cannot be the decisive criterion of mental disorder. People may be completely divorced from reality in certain ways without being considered deranged. The ancients who believed that the movement of the sun across the sky was the action of Apollo driving his fiery chariot across the heavens, or the medieval European who viewed the earth as the center of the universe, were divorced from reality, but they were not mentally disordered. Similarly, medieval people, living in a world populated by a variety of unseen creatures—ghosts, fairies, witches, leprechauns, goblins, and so on—were clearly sane, despite the fact that they were divorced from reality.

There are many reasons for misperceiving reality that have nothing to do with mental disorder. One cause may simply be ignorance; one has false conceptions of reality because one has been supplied with erroneous information. Another reason may be misinterpretation. The correct facts have been supplied but they have been misunderstood. A third is the fact that in many cases it is virtually impossible to know what the reality actually is. Is it unrealistic for me to believe that I have been treated unfairly by my professor; that the blame for my broken marriage lies with my spouse; that I deserve the feelings of guilt that I feel? In many cases we must deal more with matters of judgment than of fact. Although no one can deny that the mentally ill may hold distorted views of reality, only the omniscient do not.

Means and Ends. Rational behavior is generally viewed as behavior that employs the most effective means to attain certain ends. Actions poorly designed to achieve objectives are judged to be irrational. When an adolescent commits suicide in order to get even with his father, it is reasonable to ask whether he might not have found a less drastic way of punishing the parent. Bleuler describes cases of schizophrenics who suddenly rush to the door of the ward to escape, even though they know the door is locked, and they do so in full view of ward attendants whose task is to prevent them from leaving the ward.

Psychotic behavior often shows a poor connection between means and ends. For example, one of Bleuler's patients was constantly writing letters to people, marking them "registered mail," yet made no effort to mail them. "Many a patient consumes himself with anxiety over his imminent death but will not take the least precaution for his self-preservation and remains totally unmoved in the face of real danger to his life" (EB, pp. 64–65).

Furthermore, sane behavior may also be irrational. Normal people constantly use inappropriate means to attain their ends. En route to a given destination, one makes a wrong turn. Intent on acquiring wealth, one invests in a bad stock. Interested in defeating a chess opponent, one makes a disastrous move. If one judges the discrepancy between means and ends to be the hallmark of irrationality, then one can only say that irrationality is universal.

Consistency of Cognitive Components. A third conception of irrationality deals with the internal consistency of ideas. When people hold opposing or internally contradictory positions on certain issues, they are often described as irrational. Consider the following examples drawn from Bleuler:

> A Catholic paranoid patient had joined the Old-Catholic sect. He claimed to be persecuted by the Pope who nevertheless wanted to shower the patient with millions of dollars. (EB, p. 54)

> For weeks on end, a mother exerts every means at her command to see her child. When permission is granted her, she prefers to have a glass of wine. (EB, p. 65)

Inconsistency, however, is not the exclusive property of the mentally disordered. Contradictory ideas are to be found everywhere. As Krech and Crutchfield (1948, p. 51) express it:

> Man is not psychologically "unicellular." He is not subject to only one stimulus at a time or required to make only one response at a time. He is remarkably complex, existing at every moment in a number of simultaneous, overlapping psychological situations. . . . A man may wish to be married and, at the same time, desire not to leave his mother. He may have a need for economic security in a prosaic job and a longing for travel and adventure. He may wish to aggress against a hated rival and fear to incur the social disapproval of those who abhor aggression.

Aside from such internal psychological conflicts, inconsistency is built into the very fabric of the culture. The well-socialized, highly conformist citizen is usually full of contradictory ideas (see, for example, Lynd and Lynd 1937; Merton 1976). A person who is totally free of inconsistent or contradictory ideas walks not upon this earth.

Emotional Excess. Finally, irrationality is often associated in people's minds with emotional excess. As Hobbes (1968, p. 139) expressed it: ". . . to have stronger, and more vehement Passions for any thing, than is ordinarily seen in others, is that which men call MADNESSE."

The intensity of the phobic's response is an illustration of an emotional reaction that appears to be entirely out of proportion to the stimulus event. One person, looking at a friendly puppy, begins to tremble, breaks out in a cold sweat, and stares in terror at the animal. A woman who is afraid of storms worries for days in advance of a predicted storm. If her husband is away, she makes plans to stay overnight with a friend rather than face the storm alone. During the storm, she covers her eyes and moves away from windows in order to avoid seeing the lightning (CB, p. 199). No one would deny that these emotional responses are excessive in relation to the stimulus event.

The duration of the emotion may also be excessive (Thoits 1985, 1989). The widow's outpouring of grief, judged as appropriate at the time of the funeral, is viewed as pathological if it persists for longer than six months, according to current psychiatric criteria (DSM). Momentary anger at a snub is considered rational, but being angry at that person for the rest of one's life is not.

Although such emotionally inappropriate responses may be indicative of mental disorder, emotional excess cannot serve as its defining feature. For one thing, many psychotic symptoms have nothing to do with emotional excess. One person saves string for years on end, rolling it into larger and larger balls; another is unable to leave her room unless her clothes are arranged perfectly and her shoes are lined up in a certain way. Such behavior is judged to be disordered whatever the emotional state of the individual.

Second, emotional excess may be a product of influences that have nothing to do with mental disorder. I may shout angrily at someone I do not know because I mistakenly assume that he is my enemy. A mother may shriek at her child for some trivial misbehavior because of other severe stresses to which she is subjected. The fact that someone's emotional reaction appears to be excessive does not in itself indicate mental illness.

In sum, although the mentally disordered may exhibit such "irrational" responses, so too may perfectly normal people. The psychological concept of irrationality, like abnormality and psychological distress, cannot serve as the defining feature of mental disorder.

Psychosocial Conceptions

Psychosocial conceptions of mental disorder refer to the individual's ability to meet the ordinary demands of social life—getting along with others, fulfilling normal social responsibilities, and generally functioning effectively in life. Disorders of this type usually fall under the heading of either disability or maladjustment. Although the two concepts overlap substantially, I will use the term *disability* to refer to disturbances in social and occupational functioning, whereas the term *maladjustment* will be used to refer to disturbances in interpersonal relations.

Disability

Mentally disordered people do experience disability of one kind or another. They may have difficulty holding down a job, fulfilling family responsibilities, maintaining friendships, and so on. Even bipolar patients experiencing a manic episode—full of enthusiasm, energy, vitality, and conviviality—inevitably get into difficulty. They are likely to spend money too freely, make unwise business investments, drive recklessly, and undertake too many ambitious new projects that never get carried through to completion.

Depression may also seriously disrupt an individual's life. According to DSM–III–R (p. 221):

> In Major Depressive Episodes the degree of impairment varies, but there is always some interference in social and occupational functioning. If impairment is severe, the person may be totally unable to function socially or occupationally, or even to feed or clothe himself or herself or maintain minimal personal hygiene.

But disability cannot be considered the defining feature of mental disorder. First, certain TEBs may be disordered even if they do not interfere with normal life functioning. There are people, for example, who hear voices but are careful to conceal this fact from others. They may thus be able to hold down a job, maintain certain friendships, and function perfectly well in other ways. In some cases, disordered symptoms may actually enhance social and occupational functioning. A compulsive accountant may check his or her figures again and again, resulting in error-free performance.

Second, people may experience difficulty in social and occupational functioning for reasons that have nothing to do with mental disorder. Accident, illness, war, unemployment, inflation, racism, floods, hurricanes, and so on may all make it difficult to carry on one's social roles. If a flood washes away my place of work, I am hardly in a position to fulfill my normal occupational responsibilities. The failure to play one's usual occupational and family roles is thus not in itself indicative of mental disorder.

Maladjustment

Maladjustment, in the sense of having difficulty getting along in society, or experiencing what Szasz (1970b) has called "problems in living," often characterizes the mentally disordered. Schizophrenics often exhibit social withdrawal and may live their lives as isolates or near-isolates. Antisocial personalities usually show a long history of conflict with parents, peers, and teachers. They are, by any criterion, maladjusted. Disturbances in interpersonal relations are virtually universal among psychotics.

But maladjustment, conceived as problems in getting along with people or fitting into society, characterizes normal people as well. Criminals, revolutionaries, artists, and poets may be poorly adjusted to their societies, but they are not considered mentally ill. It might even be argued that good adjustment to bad conditions may be indicative of mental disorder (Jahoda

1958). A person who struggles against prejudice, corruption, injustice, and exploitation may be at odds with his or her society but is not considered deranged.

In sum, mentally healthy as well as mentally ill persons often have difficulty fulfilling their social and occupational roles, and otherwise adjusting satisfactorily to society. Therefore, disability and maladjustment cannot be considered defining features of mental disorder.

Medical Conceptions

Since the field of psychiatry is a branch of medicine, it characteristically views mental disorder as a disease. This is clearly evident in current psychiatric terminology. Psychiatrists refer to mental disorder as an *illness*. The clients for their services are called *patients*. The assessment of the disorder is described as a *diagnosis*. The treatment is called a *therapy*. The disorder is said to have an etiology (cause), a course, a treatment, and a cure. The therapy is provided in doctors' offices, clinics, and hospitals, and is performed by doctors, nurses, attendants, and so on (Szasz 1970b). Clearly the medical conceptual apparatus pervades psychiatry through and through.

Cockerham (1989, p. 70) has described the medical approach as follows:

> The medical model views mental disorder as a disease or diseaselike entity that can be treated through medical means. That is, the medical model attributes mental abnormalities to physiological, biochemical, or genetic causes and attempts to treat these abnormalities by way of medically grounded procedures such as psychopharmacology (drug therapy), electroshock therapy (EST), or psychosurgery (brain surgery). In this particular context, a person who is mentally ill is regarded as sick in much the same manner as if that person were physically ill.

This view has not been without its critics. For a quarter of a century Thomas Szasz (1961, 1970a, 1970b, 1987), himself a psychiatrist, has been attacking the medical approach to mental disorder. In psychiatry, he charges, illusions or bizarre behavior are treated as overt symptoms of underlying brain disorders, just as skin lesions, shortness of breath, or abnormal EKGs are viewed as overt symptoms of underlying physical disorders. However, as Szasz has pointed out, if mental illnesses were diseases of the brain, then they should be manifested in such physical responses as blindness or paralysis. But these are neurological defects, not mental disorders. Mental disorder is likely to be expressed in a belief or an idea, not in a physical lesion. A mental patient may think that he is Attila the Hun or that his enemies are sending radar waves through his body, but these are disorders of the mind, not of the brain. Szasz concludes that there is no basis for considering mental disorder to be an illness. One can only speak of mental illness in a metaphorical, not a literal, sense.

A further challenge to the medical model is Fingarette's (1972) observation that, even in the absence of any knowledge about physical pathology, judges, doctors, and other members of society have identified certain people as mentally disordered. That means that they have done so on nonbiological grounds. He states (p. 23):

> All this surely suggests, indeed it almost certainly proves, that the concepts of insanity and mental disease . . . must have a meaning and a rationale that are not tied to any specific causal or physical hypothesis at all. The meaning and rationale must be rooted deeply and widely in the ethical–legal notions of our culture, in our everyday notions of human nature and human relations, rather than a special, esoteric, or technical notion tied to some particular causal hypothesis or technical formulation.

Even if physical causes could be identified, Fingarette argues, insanity is inherently different from physical illness. It is true that recent research, making use of sophisticated medical instrumentation (CAT and PETT scans), has identified the presence of some nonspecific brain damage in 20 to 35 percent of schizophrenic patients (Seidman 1983). But that does not mean that the physical lesion is itself the defining feature of mental disorder. This is apparent when we consider some of the TEBs that are symptomatic of mental illness. One man is suspicious that people are plotting against him; another is sexually aroused by the sight of women's shoes; a third goes from doctor to doctor seeking a cure for a physical disorder that does not exist; a fourth has an irresistible impulse to set fires; a fifth explodes in a towering rage with little or no provocation.

The point is that even if biological factors were somehow found to underlie these mental symptoms, the defining feature of mental disorder— that is, the reason we judge these symptoms to be disordered—would be something other than the biological abnormality.

A key difficulty with the view of mental disorder as disease lies in the fundamentally different nature of physical and mental symptoms. For example, physical symptoms generally (though not always) mean the same thing, whoever has them. A sneeze reflects a cold, whatever one's race, religion, or ethnic origin. Certain laboratory readings may be indicative of gout, whether one is at work or at home, in school or on the street, in church or a college lecture hall.

But that is not true of mental symptoms. For example, assume that a man suddenly stands up and begins gesticulating wildly with his arms and shouting at the top of his lungs. Such behavior at most church services or college lectures might well be considered suggestive of mental disorder. But the identical behavior performed at a football game or by a person in a burning theater would be considered perfectly sane.

There are, then, fundamental differences between physical and mental symptoms. Fever, hypertension, and low red blood count are symptoms of physical disorder, no matter who has them, in what situations they appear, or what interpretation is given them. Mental symptoms, in contrast, depend on social identity, context, interpretation, and other nonmedical considerations. It is thus apparent that nonmedical factors play an important role in determining the mental health status of the symptom. Judgments of insanity do not rest solely on biological grounds.

Legal Conceptions

Anglo-Saxon law has long distinguished between criminal acts for which the individual is held responsible and those for which perpetrators are held to be not guilty by reason of insanity. Because it is difficult to establish criteria of mental disorder, this distinction has introduced a great deal of uncertainty into legal decisions.

In the landmark *M'Naghten* case in 1843, the British justices decided that a perpetrator was absolved of criminal responsibility if, at the time of the criminal act, he was unable to recognize the difference between right and wrong and was not aware that he was doing wrong (Fingarette 1972). In succeeding decades, a new criterion was introduced into the legal system: was the perpetrator, at the time of committing the criminal act, capable of controlling the behavior? A perpetrator could be absolved of criminal responsibility if the act was the result of an "irresistible impulse."

These two criteria never proved to be entirely satisfactory; doubts and uncertainties continued to surround the issue of mental illness. Finally, in 1964, the well-known *Durham* decision introduced an entirely different type of criterion. According to this ruling, an individual was absolved of criminal responsibility if the act was the result of mental illness.

How satisfactory are these three criteria in identifying the defining feature of mental disorder? The *Durham* standard, or course, is of no help at all. All it says is that a TEB is mentally ill because it is caused by mental illness. Let us therefore consider the other two.

The *M'Naghten* criterion of mental disorder is that the perpetrator, at the time of committing the crime, was unable to distinguish between good and evil. However useful this criterion may be for legal purposes, it cannot serve as the defining feature because most mental disorder has nothing to do with morality. Symptoms like the belief that one is being controlled by a dead person or that others are spying on you have nothing to do with the inability to distinguish between good and evil. TEBs may be mentally disordered whether or not moral or legal awareness is present.

The criterion of voluntary control is more complex. This criterion deals with the question of whether the perpetrator, when committing a criminal act, was unable to control its performance. There are several problems associated with this view of mental disorder. By and large, this criterion is irrelevant. When a patient holds grandiose ideas about his fame, power, and wealth, the question of his ability to exercise control over his act is irrelevant.

What do we mean when we say that a person is not in control of his or her behavior? One important school of thought denies the possibility of free will. All behavior—even that which we believe to be freely chosen—is in fact the result of deterministic forces. To reject this idea is to deny the necessity of causation.

When people say that someone is unable to control his or her behavior, they imply that powerful inner forces have governed the individual's actions against his or her own will. As Fingarette (1972) notes:

> We speak of being "overwhelmed" by passion, "dominated" by a mood or an emotion, of "surrendering" to desire, of "weakness of will," of "losing control of oneself." . . . We may find it congenial to speak idiomatically of the insane person as one who is driven, or seized, or overwhelmed, or possessed by fear, anxiety, emotions, or delusions. Yet there is one literal truth we must never lose sight of: it is the person himself who initiates and carries out the deed. It is his desire, his mood, his passion, his belief which is at issue, and it is he who acts to satisfy this desire or to express this mood, emotion, or belief of his. Even if his motive is unconscious, it is his motive, and it is he who acts out of this motive. (pp. 159, 162)

The idea of loss of voluntary control is thus extremely blurry. Can I say that I am guiltless of the crime, and that the blame should be assigned entirely to my strong feeling? Do we say that a smoker is not responsible for smoking, that it is the "inner force" of habit that is guilty? Do we say that the jealous husband is free of legal responsibility, that it is his jealousy that must be found guilty? It is not surprising that this criterion of insanity has so often proved to be unsatisfactory in courts of law. As a candidate to represent the defining feature of mental disorder in general, it is even less satisfactory.

Interactional Conceptions

Interactional theories are those that locate the defining feature of mental disorder in the social intercourse of human beings. Here I wish to consider one such theory: the theory of nonverbal communication.

Nonverbal Communication

In setting forth their theory of mental disorder as a problem in nonverbal communication, Miller and Jaques (1988) begin with the proposition that the continued existence of society depends on human cooperation. In order to ensure that the essential tasks of society are performed, people must work together productively. But this is only possible if the social encounters are harmonious and successful.

The most essential feature of successful social interaction is communication. Such communication can be verbal or "nonverbal, contextual, or connotative" (Miller and Jaques 1988, p. 276). The core of Miller and Jaques's theory is that "it is problems in nonverbal communication that cause the psychotic to damage or disrupt social encounters" (p. 276).

The success of social encounters, Miller and Jaques contend, depends on people's use of a common frame of reference with respect to the use of time and space. Deviation from the accepted spatiotemporal rules disrupts the social encounter. Violations of spatial norms include invading the listener's personal space (e.g., getting too close when speaking) and stepping back physically, gazing in the wrong direction, and turning away when speaking or listening. Examples of temporal rule violation are failure to observe the rules of turn-taking, speaking too quickly or too slowly, pausing too long, and so on.

On the basis of both empirical observation and theoretical analysis, Miller and Jaques (1988, p. 278) conclude:

> It is now possible to be specific about the kinds of deviation that cause people to be labeled as psychologically disturbed. They entail the use of time and space, predominantly in nonverbal communication, and in a manner that damages the social encounter.

It is clear that many psychotics do exhibit the spatiotemporal patterns reported by Miller and Jaques. Bleuler (EB, p. 37) noted in his studies of schizophrenics that there was often "great irregularity in association time. . . . Frequently striking changes occur, at times the associations go very slowly; then suddenly one sees the patient can think very rapidly (in the same experiment, of course)."

Since Miller and Jaques explicitly limit their theory to schizophrenia, it is not possible to assess its applicability to other forms of mental disorder. In any event, there is ample reason to question its serviceability as the defining feature of schizophrenia.

First, consider their contention that schizophrenia is characterized by disturbances in nonverbal communication. But what about verbal communication? Surely, no one would deny that verbal communications are relevant to schizophrenia. The flight of ideas, irrelevant associations, incoherence, and verbalized delusional systems are all classic symptoms of schizophrenia. Even if problems in nonverbal communication did exist, one could not say that schizophrenia was present when these problems were present and absent when they were absent.

Furthermore, most of the symptoms of schizophrenia have nothing to do with the misuse of time and space. When schizophrenics believe that secret forces are persecuting them; that people are inserting thoughts in their heads; that the television announcer is making fun of them—what do these thoughts have to do with the violation of spatiotemporal rules?

In addition, the disruption of social encounters may stem from many causes other than the violation of spatiotemporal rules. Hatred, resentment, jealousy, insult, ignorance, anger, competition, misunderstanding, false information, perspectival differences—all these and more may disrupt or even destroy social encounters. For example, Goffman (1955) has vividly described a number of rule violations that may endanger social encounters. In any interaction, he points out, people must accept one another's presented selves and must act as if they believe them to be authentic. Each party must protect the self of the other, a process that may demand false affirmations, concealment, avoidance, disclaimers, and other ploys designed to maintain successful social interaction. Serious threats to social encounters are a prominent and pervasive feature of normal human interaction.

Finally, many of the TEBs that are judged to be mentally disordered have little or nothing to do with the disruption of social encounters. Hearing voices, seeing visions, lacking affect, holding strange ideas—all this is evidence of mental illness independent of their effect on social interaction. It is thus evident that many disturbances in social encounters are not due to mental illness and that many mentally ill TEBs do not involve social encounters. This conception cannot serve as the defining feature of schizophrenia, let alone mental disorder generally.

Societal Reaction Conceptions

Whereas the conceptions of mental disorder presented so far anchor insanity either in the individual psyche or in the individual's social relationships, societal reaction theories locate mental disorder in processes of social definition. In these views, it is not the TEB as such but the societal response to it that is the crucial issue.

For example, in the past, psychiatry viewed homosexuality as a mental disorder. With the rise of the Gay Rights Movement, however, the American Psychiatric Association altered its view on the subject. What had changed was not the nature of the individual's sexual preference but the social definition of it. Similarly, people who saw visions in medieval society were sometimes hailed as saints, whereas in our society this behavior is likely to be judged as psychotic. In the view of the societal reaction theorists, then, TEBs are not mentally disordered in themselves. What makes them mentally disordered is the fact that they are so defined by society.

In this discussion, I would like to consider three societal reaction theories of mental disorder: labeling theory, social control theory, and emotional deviance theory. These theories, although closely related, nevertheless have certain distinctive features. The first sees the defining feature of mental illness to be the outcome of social classification; the second, a moral verdict passed on hapless victims; and the third, an instance of a particular kind of social norm violation.

Labeling Theory

Labeling theory was introduced into sociology as a new way of thinking about such deviant behavior as crime and delinquency (Lemert 1951, 1972; Becker 1963; Schur 1971; Erikson 1962). Earlier studies of deviance had focused largely on efforts to understand the social and psychological characteristics of individuals that fostered deviance. The innovative feature of labeling theory was to shift the focus away from the deviant and toward the societal reaction to the deviance. Rather than asking, What made the delinquent behave the way he did? the labeling theorist substituted the question: Why did society judge the behavior to be delinquent, and what were the consequences of this societal judgment?

The labeling approach to the explanation of delinquency begins with the assumption that some deviant behavior is normal. At one time or another, most youngsters will scrawl graffiti on walls, steal hubcaps, pilfer from stores, and get involved in gang fights. In most cases, nothing happens as a result of this behavior, and it is gradually abandoned as the children grow older. On occasion, however, some youngsters are apprehended. Whether or not they are may be a matter of chance—they get "caught"— or may stem from police stereotypes about minorities or lower-class youngsters. Whatever the reason, these children may be brought to the police station, their names entered on the police record, and they may even be brought before a judge. When found guilty, the child is officially labeled a delinquent (even if the sentence is suspended). He now has a "record."

This labeling process has fateful consequences for the individual. No longer will a youngster, for example, be regarded, like his peers, as a "wild kid." He is now formally identified as a lawbreaker. Other people—parents, teachers, classmates—treat him as such. Parents urge their straight male and female offspring to steer clear of him; teachers keep him at arm's length. At the same time he is recruited into the delinquent gang and gains a newfound approbation from this source. These experiences bring into being an altered self-image. The youngster no longer sees himself as just a daring, fun-loving kid; he now identifies himself as a delinquent. Since he, like everyone else, has internalized the social stereotype of what delinquents are like, he proceeds to behave in accordance with these social expectations, that is, to play the role of a delinquent.

According to Lemert (1951, p. 76), the primary deviance has now become secondary deviance. Even though his initial behavior may have been no different from that of most of his peers, a major consequence of the labeling process itself is to change his self-image and, consequently, his behavior, and to launch him on a criminal career.

There is little doubt that this is a powerful theory, one that has greatly enhanced our understanding of delinquent and criminal behavior. Thomas Scheff (1966, 1974, 1984) has extended this theory to the explanation of mental disorder. His theory has become the preeminent sociological theory of mental illness.

Scheff, like Lemert, contends that in the ordinary course of events most people exhibit certain kinds of behavior that violate social norms. In most cases these behaviors (like the delinquent behavior of adolescents) are overlooked and their importance dismissed. In a small proportion of cases, however—perhaps based on accident or on stereotypes associated with racial minorities or lower-class behavior—attention is drawn to these normative violations. People may respond to this behavior by calling the police, or by bringing the individual to the emergency room, the doctor's office, or the mental hospital. Once one of these certifying agents designate the individual as mentally ill, a series of events is set in motion that transforms the primary deviance into secondary deviance. Other people's attitudes and behavior toward the individual are radically transformed. Employers, spouses, co-workers, and relatives no longer look on the individual as "slightly peculiar" or as "a character." They now reconstruct history to fit the individual's past behavior into the stereotype of insanity which they have learned in the culture. The labeled individual, discovering that both the official agents of society (doctors, courts) and the people he knows well consider him to be mentally ill, internalizes this social definition. Guided by the stereotypes of insanity that he or she has learned in the course of socialization, the individual proceeds to act out the sick person's role. "Most mental disorder," according to Scheff (1966, p. 54), "can be considered a social role."

Although labeling theory has generated a great deal of interest among sociologists, it has also been subjected to a number of criticisms (e.g., Gove 1970, 1980, 1982; Cockerham 1989). One criticism relates to Scheff's description of the *processes* involved in the designation of a person as insane. It is Scheff's contention that members of society learn certain stereotypes of insanity, usually in childhood, and that they come to identify as insane those people whose thoughts, emotions, and behaviors match these stereotypes. In time, according to Scheff, the individual who has been labeled as mentally disordered internalizes these social definitions and behaves in a fashion consistent with these social expectations.

But Scheff offers little more than a hint of what this social stereotype of insanity might be. The closest he comes to describing it is to cite Nunnally's description of the mass media's portrayal of the insane (e.g., "glassy-eyed, with his mouth widely ajar, mumbling incoherent phrases and laughing uncontrollably") (Scheff 1966, p. 68).

The argument that people are classified as mentally disordered because their behavior matches the social stereotype of insanity is flawed because people's stereotypes of the mentally disordered tend to be wrong. As noted earlier, studies of public attitudes toward the mentally ill (Halpert 1970; Nunnally 1961) show that most people tend to think of the insane as unpredictable and dangerous. But, as Scheff himself stresses, such behavior is not at all characteristic of the mentally disordered. If, as Scheff claims, mentally ill persons were behaving in accordance with the social stereotypes of insanity, then their actual behavior would be very different; in other words, they would give very unauthentic role performances. Nor does Scheff provide an iota of evidence to show that this stereotype, or any other accurate stereotype, is learned and internalized in childhood. The only person who might be expected to behave in terms of the social stereotype would be a mentally sane person feigning insanity.

Another reason to question this view is the enormous diversity of thought, feeling, and behavior of the mentally disordered. If mental disorder represented the playing of a social role, as Scheff avers, then most mentally ill people would manifest *similar* behavior, since presumably they are acting in accordance with a shared social stereotype. In Scheff's (1966, p. 82) words, the behavior of the person labeled mentally ill becomes "similar to the behavior of other deviants classified as mentally ill." In fact, however, the thoughts, emotions, and behaviors of the mentally disordered are almost infinitely varied. The schizophrenic shows little similarity to the psychopathic personality. The psychosexual deviate does not act like the obsessive–compulsive. The panic disorder has little in common with the depressive episode. Any reasonably complete description of the range of mental symptoms (e.g., DSM) shows that the typical behavior of people with different disorders probably varies as widely as the behavior of sane persons.

There is no social stereotype that can possibly encompass this enormous behavioral diversity. Even within a single diagnostic category—schizophrenia—the behavior can be astoundingly different. Some schizophrenics hear voices or see visions. Others speak in such a way that it is difficult to follow their train of thought. Still others display peculiar grimaces or contorted postures. Some stare at walls or appear to be devoid of emotion. And so on.

If the TEBs of schizophrenics are so varied, how much more varied is the behavior that characterizes the full range of mental disorders? A phobic is afraid to go out into the street or ride an elevator. An obsessive keeps thinking about the same thing all the time. A compulsive constantly washes her hands. People with somatoform disorders think that every ache and pain is a fatal disease; as a result, they spend their lives going from doctor to doctor in a futile effort to deal with their imaginary ailments. A person experiencing a depressive episode looks, acts, and feels exactly the opposite of someone experiencing a manic episode. A single disorder may even be expressed in symptoms that are exactly the reverse of one another. For example, major depression includes symptoms of eating too much and eating too little and sleeping too much and sleeping too little. (DSM, p. 222)

In sum, there is no social stereotype that could possibly match this enormous diversity of thought, emotion, or behavior. Scheff's contention that mental illness is a social role—that the mentally disordered are behaving in accordance with the social stereotype which has been internalized in the course of socialization—is a logical impossibility.

Furthermore, this contention implies a level of social docility that is impossible to accept (Rotenberg 1974). The penalties that people must pay for being defined as mentally ill—loss of freedom, civil liberties, career, family, friends, and so many other sources of pleasure in life—are enormous. Is it likely that anyone would accept such deprivation without demur? Surely people are not so docile or so well socialized as Scheff's theory seems to imply.

Another question that can be raised about Scheff's theory concerns its pivotal concept of residual deviance. According to Scheff (1966, pp. 33–34):

> The culture of the group provides a vocabulary of terms for categorizing many norm violations: crime, perversion, drunkenness, and bad manners are familiar examples. Each of these terms is derived from the type of norm broken, and ultimately, from the type of behavior involved. After exhausting these categories, however, there is always a residue of the most diverse kinds of violations, for which the culture provides no explicit label. . . .
> In this discussion, the diverse kinds of rule-breaking for which our society provides no explicit label, and which, therefore, sometimes leads to the labeling of the violator as mentally ill, will be considered technically *residual rule-breaking*.

Although this argument seems plausible, when one examines it more carefully, one finds it to be extraordinarily vague, open-ended, and all-encompassing. What constitutes a residual rule and how can one tell whether it has been violated? When a man tells us that the television announcer is making fun of him, is he thereby violating a residual rule? If so, which one? Is there a social rule against believing that one is Joan of Arc or Albert Einstein? Is the problem with refusal to sit in a chair because it is yellow the fact that one has violated some social rule? Does an obsessional worry about germs represent the violation of a left-over rule? Surely, the problem in these instances is not that some social rule has been violated. Something quite different must be involved.

Labeling theory is also subject to other criticisms; some of these will be considered in Chapter 4. But even this limited discussion makes it apparent that social labeling cannot serve as the defining feature of mental disorder.

Social Control Theory

Building on the work of Scheff, Sarbin and Mancuso (1980) have set forth a societal reaction theory that views labeling as an instrument of social control. Scheff had argued that the label of mental disorder is assigned to individuals on the basis of happenstance or, perhaps, negative stereotypes associated with class, race, or ethnic status. Sarbin and Mancuso have carried this theory one step further by suggesting that the assignment of the label has a *social purpose*. In their view the purpose of labeling is to control the behavior of nonconforming members of society.

Conformity to social rules, they note, is essential for the continued existence of society. Society selectively applies the label of mental illness as a way of ensuring such conformity. To call a person mentally ill is like calling him or her a witch, a red, an unmarried mother, and so on. Such negative epithets (or identities) are assigned to people who violate social norms. According to Sarbin and Mancuso (1980, p. 220):

> Designations of disrespect and lack of esteem are used as a first step toward controlling the conduct of degraded persons. A society manages to employ a variety of instrumental and ritual actions to control or contain conduct: execution, banishment, sequestering, incarceration, flogging, reprimanding, shaming, and branding. The tradition that has supported schizophrenia as diagnosis is one of many traditions arising from society's need to control its nonconforming members. That schizophrenia has become a euphemism for unwanted or unwelcome conduct cannot be gainsaid. . . . Schizophrenia is a moral verdict masquerading as a medical diagnosis.

The assignment of the schizophrenic label is especially likely to occur, Sarbin and Mancuso contend, if the behavior threatens the established power structure. "If the acts place the significant (and usually more powerful) others at risk, the person is likely to be declared unfit, crazy, and dangerous" (p. 220). The application of the nonperson label to the schizophrenic is thus a way that entrenched interests use to subdue threats to their position.

Of course, Sarbin and Mancuso point out, that is not the way it appears on the surface. Schizophrenics are described as "sick" and are placed in mental hospitals in order to "treat" and "cure" them. But, in reality, they contend, the real purpose is to punish and control those people who violate the social rules and threaten the established social order.

I believe that Sarbin and Mancuso are correct in viewing insanity as a threat to the social order. One of the main pillars of the social order is the normative system of society. Unless people generally observe the rules and practices of society, society would rapidly disintegrate. These norms pervade all aspects of social life. Schizophrenics speak or act in ways that are socially inappropriate and thereby disturb the effective functioning of society. In this sense, insanity does represent a threat to the social order.

But this is not the same as saying that the label of schizophrenic is applied to these people for the *purpose* of punishing and controlling them. First of all, where is the threat? Sarbin and Mancuso offer no evidence—nor am I aware of any—to suggest that insane people are any more likely than sane ones to attack the power structure. Second, it is difficult to see in what way most of the symptoms of psychosis threaten the power structure. How does hearing voices, having visions, avoiding elevators, stopping in the middle of a sentence pose a threat to the power structure? Third, how does labeling, or even threatening to label someone a schizophrenic deter him or her from hearing voices, seeing visions, or speaking incoherently? Surely these things must happen whether or not society threatens to call them schizophrenic. There may be some occasions when people desist from expressing opinions because they fear they will be labeled insane, but this must be one of the least common reasons why people inhibit the expression of their ideas. There is little or no foundation for the social control theory of schizophrenia.

Emotional Deviance Theory

In 1985, Peggy Thoits challenged Scheff's labeling theory on the following grounds: If mental disorder were attributable to labeling, then how could one explain the fact that people could classify *themselves* as mentally disordered? Thoits pointed out that many people judged *themselves* to be mentally ill, even though society had not applied this label to them.

Thoits (1985) proposed a different view of mental disorder. She suggested that people label themselves as mentally disordered when they exhibit emotional deviance. Every society, she noted, is characterized by a system of normatively prescribed emotions. People are taught that it is socially appropriate to feel certain emotions on certain occasions or when playing certain social roles. "We know what we should feel in a variety of circumstances (e.g., sad at a funeral, lively at a party, happy at a wedding, proud on success, angry at an insult, and so on). Although these rules usually are not codified formally, they are learned and repeatedly reinforced in social interaction" (p. 224). This is true, incidentally, of the emotions we feel (emotional experience) as well as the emotions we show (emotional display).

Emotional deviance theory is considered a societal reaction theory of mental disorder because it is rooted in the social norms. It is the violation of these emotional norms, according to Thoits, that induces people to seek psychiatric care. There is, however, reason to question whether this is the defining feature of mental disorder.

First of all, there are many cognitive and behavioral problems that are just as characteristic of mental illness as emotional ones. Second, people may display emotional deviance without being considered mentally ill. A person who feels insufficient joy at a wedding may be puzzled but would hardly call into question his own sanity. People often find themselves exploding with fury at some outrage, or feeling intense nervousness before some important event, but do not ordinarily seek admission to a mental hospital on these grounds. The violation of emotional rules, then, as I will show later, is rarely judged to be indicative of mental illness.

Discussion

It is thus apparent that there is no dearth of ideas about the nature of mental disorder. The general public, psychiatrists, psychologists, sociologists, philosophers, legal theorists, and others have all contributed to this abundance. I have discussed popular conceptions, psychological conceptions, psychosocial conceptions, medical conceptions, legal conceptions, interactional conceptions, and societal reaction conceptions of mental disorder. None of these has succeeded in identifying the defining feature of mental disorder. In saying this, I do not mean to suggest that many of these features may not be *characteristic* of mental disorder; in fact, later in this work I shall attempt to explain why these features are actually more likely to characterize mentally ill than normal people. In many cases the propagators of these theories tend to be descriptively right, but for the wrong reasons.

The argument I advance in this book is that the defining feature of mental disorder is the occurrence of role-taking failure (Rosenberg 1984). Role-taking failure is a societal reaction theory of mental disorder. Like labeling, social control, and emotional deviance theories, it anchors the disorder not in the individual but in the response of society to the individual's TEBs. My basic argument is that what makes thoughts, emotions, and behaviors mentally disordered is the fact that the observer is unable to take the role of the actor.

I do not mean, of course, that a single instance of role-taking failure will usually suffice to elicit the judgment of insanity. This judgment will almost always depend on the nature, severity, and duration of the symptom, as well as other factors. But the basic point is the same: We view a person as insane if we cannot understand certain thought, emotion, or behavior that is manifested repeatedly, intensely, or over an extended period of time.

In order to lay the foundation for this theory, it is first necessary to delve more deeply into the nature of role-taking. What is it? How does it develop? Are people born with the ability to take the role of the other? What accounts for the universality of the phenomenon? After I have addressed these and related questions, I will then compare role-taking theory with the various conceptions of mental disorder described in this chapter.

2
Role-Taking Failure: A Theory of Mental Disorder

Sociologists often equate the concept of role-taking with role playing, role performance, or role enactment. A role, in the latter sense, is a set of prescriptions for behavior attached to a social position. People are said to be playing a role when they are acting in accordance with the social expectations attached to the position. In order to play one's role, one must also learn the social expectations attached to the roles of other persons linked to one's "role-set" (Merton 1957). For example, nurses cannot play their own roles properly unless they are familiar with the doctor's role.

But sociologists also use the term *role-taking* in a somewhat different sense. As Heiss (1981, pp. 29–30) observes:

> The terms "taking the role of the other," "taking the attitude of the other," and "role-taking" all refer to the same human capacity—the ability to put oneself in the place of others through the use of imagination, to see things with their eyes.

Role-taking in this sense goes beyond simply understanding the social expectations associated with a social position. What is involved in role-taking is the *attempt to look into the mind of another human being*. Were it not for the unfortunate connotations of the term, the process might better be described as "mind-reading." Unfortunately, this term cannot be used because the dictionary defines mind-reading as "the professed ability to discern the thoughts of others without the normal means of communication, esp. by means of an alleged preternatural power." For want of a better term, I have opted to use Hartley and Hartley's (1952) term, "thought-reading." To take the role of the other is to attempt to probe the other person's thoughts, to penetrate the recesses of the other's mind. It involves "trying to make accurate guesses about the covert psychological processes of other people . . ." (Flavell 1968, p. v).

In focusing on this aspect of human cognition, two preliminary observations are necessary. First, when I speak of entering the mind of another person, I mean *attempting* to get inside that person's head. In the final analysis, the mind of a human being is barred to the direct gaze of any other

30

person. Role-taking, then, is the attempt, not the demonstrated success, in grasping the internal thoughts and feelings of other people.

Second, role-taking is an inferential process often characterized by a high degree of uncertainty. We can never be completely sure about what another person is actually thinking or feeling. For this reason, our inferences about other people's internal mental events tend to be working hypotheses, held tentatively, and subject to rapid revision. For example, assuming that a man enjoys humor, we tell a joke. But when we perceive the expression of distaste on his face, we conclude that our assumption was in error; we were not aware that he disliked this type of joke. Initial assumptions about the contents of others' minds are thus frequently altered in the course of social interaction.

The Discovery of Mind

It is, of course, apparent that role-taking is not always successful. Let me begin with a simple example of defective role-taking. While walking toward my car one morning, my neighbor's four-year-old boy, named Rafael, came running up to me in a state of great excitement to inform me that "Benjy just had a bath." What is interesting is that Rafael *failed to take my role,* as evidenced by his obliviousness to my own thought processes. He did not consider the fact that I did not know who Benjy was (it turned out to be the family dog) or that this event did not arouse in me the excitement that it did in him.

Note how different this is from most adult communication. When adults speak, they tend to take into account the listener's fund of knowledge or characteristic interests. Because I was better able to take the role of Rafael, I did *not* share with him the thoughts that were uppermost in my mind at the time, that is, I did not ask him his opinion of the Supreme Court ruling that had been reported on the morning news.

Development of Role-Taking Abilities

My experience with Rafael suggests that, in the early stages of life, role-taking is not a prominent feature of the individual's behavioral repertoire. On the contrary, role-taking appears to be part of a slow and gradual developmental process. One of the most firmly grounded postulates of genetic epistemology is the fact that young children, although not completely excluded from the role-taking process, are nevertheless less inclined or able to enter the minds of other human beings. This is what we mean when we call children "egocentric." When Piaget (1932) described children as egocentric, he meant that they see the world from their own viewpoint, not from the viewpoint of others.

It is clear that young children are relatively oblivious to the internal mental events of other persons. The little boy may learn that leaving his toys around the living room causes his mother to shriek, but he is totally ignorant of the thoughts and feelings that are the causes of her behavior. He is unaware that her reaction may stem from her fear that someone will trip over the toys, or that she might feel embarrassed if someone came in, or that toys in the living room annoy her husband, or any of a hundred other possible reasons. Even when the mother patiently explains the reason for her reaction, the explanation is likely to fall on deaf ears. The young child, while responsive to her overt behavior (e.g., shouting, spanking), has little awareness of the internal world of thought and feeling that underlies her reaction.

We thus see why studies clearly document the fact that, whereas younger children tend to focus primarily on the *social exteriors* of human beings (e.g., appearance, behavior), older children focus more on their *psychological interiors* (e.g., thought, feeling) (Rosenberg 1986a; Damon and Hart 1988; Secord and Peevers 1974). In her summary of the findings of a large body of developmental literature, Shantz (1975) concludes that "there is a developmental trend toward conceiving of people less in terms of surface appearance, possessions and motor behavior, and more in terms of an underlying reality . . . [such as] values, beliefs, and intentions" (p. 314). Thus, when the young child is asked to describe his uncle, he will talk about his height; asked to describe a teacher, she will talk about the colors the teacher wears; asked to tell us about a neighbor, she will talk about the funny hats he wears; and so on. Children also tend to describe people in terms of their overt behavior: "He gives me candy"; "he drives a big car"; "she bakes cherry pies." At this developmental stage, what commands the child's attention are things that are public, overt, and visible. Little thought is given to such questions as; What is the other person thinking? What does the other person want? What does the other person feel?

Although there is some limited awareness of the internal worlds of other people during the early years (Damon and Hart 1988), it is not until middle or late childhood that a full-fledged interest emerges. It is at these later stages that the child makes a serious effort to ascertain the thoughts of other people, to discover their feelings, and to take account of their values, motives, meanings, and attitudes (Livesley and Bromley 1973; Secord and Peevers 1974; Broughton 1978).

The question is; What brings about this shift from the virtually exclusive attention to others' social exteriors to an awareness of, and interest in, their psychological interiors? The answer, according to Piaget (1928), is social interaction and social cooperation. When the child enters school and begins to participate in games, an understanding of others' perspectives becomes essential. In multiplayer games, a child may wish to play X, but her companion may wish to play Y. This inevitably draws to the child's attention the fact that another viewpoint exists and that it is necessary to take account of it in one's intercourse with the environment. Cooperation, as Piaget (1948) points out, forces "the individual to be constantly occupied with the point of view of other people." (p. 187). When the child comes to participate in organized games, Mead (1934) has pointed out, the viewpoints of all players must be adopted. Slowly, in response to such social interaction, egocentricity declines and an awareness emerges that other people have different points of view.

Five Fundamental Discoveries

In the course of maturation and experience, children make five fundamental discoveries which remain with them for the rest of their lives:

1. The discovery that others' behavior has major effects on their lives. The satisfaction of their needs and wishes, infants learn, depends on whether the mother provides them with a bottle, hugs them, changes them, and so on, or whether, on the contrary, she spanks, frustrates, or ignores them. Early in life, children acquire the basic awareness that most of what they want out of life depends on the behavior of other people.

2. The discovery that people have minds. This insight, as noted above, develops slowly. In the early years, children are chiefly interested in, and aware of, the visible actions and overt physical characteristics of people. It is only as a result of interaction with others that children come to discover the existence of internal mental events in other people.

3. The discovery that people's mental events largely govern their behavior. To the young child, other people's behavior exists as a fact of life. It is not until children become aware of a psychological interior in other people that they come to realize that the primary causes of people's actions are to be found in these internal mental events.

4. The discovery that others' minds can be intentionally controlled. Although the sense of efficacy—of having intended effects on the environment—appears in infancy, it is not until the child discovers that others have minds that they come to realize that they can produce intended effects on those minds.

5. The discovery that the control of others' thoughts and feelings is the most important method of controlling others' actions. Such control, in turn, affects their own lives in profound and pervasive ways.

As these discoveries gradually enter children's awareness, they become increasingly interested in, and concerned with, the internal mental events of other human beings. A host of questions arise. What are other people thinking? What do they know? What are their feelings? What are their intentions? What are their perceptions? What are their opinions, attitudes, and values? What are their motives? The attempt to enter other people's thoughts, once started, becomes a major activity of the child and continues undiminished throughout the remainder of his or her life.

Role-Taking Benefits

The fact that children become so deeply engaged and highly involved in the role-taking process suggests that they have discovered that the process provides important benefits. In this discussion I want to focus on five significant benefits that accrue to people as a consequence of role-taking. These are prediction, comprehension, communication, interaction, and control.

Prediction

Human beings, according to Swann (1983, p. 34), have "an inborn preference for things that are predictable, familiar, stable, and uncertainty reducing." Life in an unpredictable world is filled with anxiety. Even noxious events are less threatening if they are predictable. For example, if a teacher shrieks all the time, the children come to expect this behavior and to adapt to it, thereby depriving these shrieks of much of their frightening quality.

In the course of maturation, children learn that they can greatly improve their predictions of others' behavior by discovering the thoughts underlying their actions. By learning about other people's likes, dislikes, attitudes, values, beliefs, interests, cognitive tendencies, emotional dispositions, and other internal events, they are in a much better position to anticipate accurately how others will respond in various situations or under different circumstances.

In the absence of thought-reading, the chief basis for predicting people's behavior is extrapolation from past events. When children are able to grasp other people's points of view, they discover that understanding *why* people act as they do greatly improves their ability to predict *whether* they will act in certain ways. Predictability thus helps to create a more stable, secure world for the child.

Comprehension

It is not always necessary to understand why people act as they do in order to deal effectively with them. If I can confidently predict that my mother will prepare breakfast in the morning, it is not necessary for me to understand the motives and sentiments that underlie her behavior.

But, as they mature, children develop an innate or conditioned desire to know *why* things happen, particularly why other people act as they do. According to Harold Kelley (1967), the motive behind such attribution is the wish to make sense of one's world. States of bafflement, puzzlement, or incomprehensibility produce emotions ranging from slight uneasiness to intense anxiety.

Role-taking locates the child in a much more comprehensible world. When the child discovers the difference between a spanking administered for his or her own good and one inflicted as a punishment for evil, then the seemingly inconsistent behavior of a loving parent is reconciled with the painful experience. When the child understands the difference between a playmate shoving in jest and one shoving in anger, actions like these come to acquire a different meaning and elicit a different response.

The enhancement of comprehension is also highly adaptive for the child. If we understand that another person's attitude and intent are hostile we develop defensive tactics to ward off the danger. On the other hand, if we judge them to be benign, we may take advantage of the opportunities offered by that feeling. If we are to adapt successfully in life, it is not enough to know how people act; it is also necessary to know what they think.

Communication

Human beings have the ability to experience a rich communicative life—to share the contents of one another's minds. Without communication there can be no social life, and without social life the prospects for species survival are extremely slim (Rosenberg 1988).

Role-taking is an essential component of the communication process. When people communicate, they must take account of the listener's thoughts and feelings and construct their verbal messages accordingly. Indeed, one of the most important differences between child and adult speech is precisely the level of role-taking activity. Unlike their seniors, young children tend to speak for the pleasure of talking, not for the purpose of producing effects on the mind of the listener. Older children and adults know that the listener has an internal world of thought and feeling, and they keep this world in mind when they speak. To communicate successfully, people must be able to answer certain questions about the psychological interiors of other people. Among these questions are the following:

1. What do other people know? What are their informational needs?
2. What are their intentions? What are they attempting to accomplish by their actions or their words?
3. What do they want? What are their motives or wishes?
4. What do they care about? What are their values?
5. What do they believe? What are their opinions, attitudes, and beliefs?

Adolescents and adults constantly take account of such questions in constructing their verbal messages. This process becomes clear when we compare adolescent and adult message construction with the verbal behavior of children, whose messages are relatively unaffected by concern with their listeners' thoughts and feelings.

Information Needs. Flavell's (1968) investigations provide striking evidence of children's neglect of their listeners' information needs.

1. Asked to give visual instructions to a blindfolded person and a sighted person, the younger children give similar instructions to both, whereas the older children give different instructions to the blindfolded person and the sighted person.
2. Asked to give directions to someone who knows an area well and to someone who does not, adolescents provide different instructions, whereas younger children give essentially the same instructions to both.
3. Asked how a child and an adult would respond to a word-association test, the younger children tend to predict that they would respond in the same way, whereas the adolescents predict that they would respond differently.

On the basis of these findings, Flavell (1968, p. 95) concludes that "the ability to tailor message content to listener needs does . . . increase with age across middle childhood and adolescence."

In the course of daily interaction, adults constantly take account of what their listeners know when they fashion their messages. When I come home from work in the evening, I do not begin by informing my spouse of my name and occupation. I do not tell my graduate students who George Herbert Mead was (since I fear I would be insulting their intelligence), but I do convey this information to my undergraduates (assuming more limited knowledge on their part). If I meet a stranger on a plane, I do not open the conversation with the question, "Do you think Harry will get into law school?" In order to fashion a message, I must look into the other's mind and judge what is there. Clearly, it is impossible to conduct a fruitful conversation without considering the informational needs of the listener.

Intentions. In speaking to others, we must take account of what they are trying to accomplish by their speech or action. If someone strides rapidly toward us, is her purpose to help us or to hurt us? If someone gives us unsolicited advice, are they acting in our interests, or are they just trying to display their knowledge (or our ignorance)? Inferences about the internal events that underlie audible words or overt actions take account of what the speaker is trying to accomplish.

Motives. The messages we construct are influenced by the motives we impute to others. One motive is the desire to protect and enhance self-esteem. Young children do not enter others' inner worlds, and so tend to be remarkably oblivious to the self-esteem needs of other people. One child may call another "stupid" or "fatso" or "weird," or explicitly inform the child he or she is no good and can't play on the team. To adults, such behavior appears astonishingly unkind. But that is not the case. It simply means that young children pay little or no attention to the needs, sensitivities, or motives of others; hence, they express what is on their minds. A child overhears his parents groan about the "boring old couple" they have invited for the evening and greets the guests with the question; "Are you the boring old couple?"

Contrast such statements with those of adults. Adults are often keenly sensitive to the self-esteem needs of their listeners. A woman does not reject a man by telling him that he is an incredible bore. Rather she tells him that she is already engaged, or that she must study for an important test that night, and so on. Being keenly aware of one another's sensitivity to slights or insults, adults devise a wide variety of euphemisms to protect the self-esteem of their conversational partners. Instead of telling someone we think he is a plodder, we tell him he is conscientious. Instead of calling someone stingy, we say he is thrifty. Instead of calling the individual stupid for failing a test, we call the test unfair or absurd (Rosenberg 1986b). The messages we fashion, then, are heavily influenced by our assumptions about other people's needs or motives.

Interests. Egocentric and sociocentric speakers differ in the degree to which they take account of their listeners' interests when speaking. When a little girl, in a burst of generosity, hands us her furry animal, she is at once demonstrating the depth of her affection and her obliviousness to our own interests. Adults, on the other hand, are more apt to be attentive to the interests of their auditors. After all, we do not reciprocate the child's generous gift of its favorite toy by handing her our latest stock market report. Nor do we tell the checkout clerk about the caustic review of our latest professional paper. When we talk to people, we constantly take account of what messages will or will not interest the particular listener.

Beliefs, Attitudes, and Values. Effective message construction obliges us to take account of the other person's beliefs, attitudes, and values. If a man erroneously assumes that his neighbor is a bigot and, on that basis, expresses a racist sentiment, he may inflict severe damage on an otherwise congenial relationship. It is for this reason that people are usually careful to avoid offending one another's religious beliefs or other sacred values. We also adapt our political messages to the listener's putative attitudes. If I want to promote a particular candidate, I may point out to a liberal how much she helps the disadvantaged, and tell a conservative how much she opposes taxes. In speaking to a religious fundamentalist, I am likely to construct a different message than when talking to a confirmed atheist. The messages we convey to people are thus heavily influenced by our assumptions about their beliefs, attitudes, and values.

The range of internal mental events that we must consider in speaking to other people is thus enormous. According to Flavell (1970, p. 1027), effective message construction must take account of "the other's perceptual experiences; his cognitive experiences, predispositions, and capacities; his emotional states; his motives and intentions—in short anything that people might construe to be a potentially 'readable' or 'inferable' entity."

If, in conversation, we paid no attention to what other people knew, what they wanted, what interested them, what inspired them, what they felt, what they believed, what they cared about—if we completely ignored these matters and spoke only from our own viewpoints—we would so confuse, baffle, antagonize, irritate, bore, or offend the listener that the conversation would quickly come to a halt. Children speak that way because they have little or no interest in what others think; but if adults are to maintain successful relationships, it is impossible for them to ignore one another's internal events.

Enrichment of Social Relationships

Role-taking also brings about a qualitative change in the nature of social relationships. Flavell (1968, p. 54) has called attention to some of the changes that can occur.

First, role-taking results in genuine, rather than apparent, interaction with peers. As role-taking skills improve, role-taking comes to be characterized by what Selman (1980) has called "mutual perspectivism." At this stage, "each person is seen as capable of taking into account the other's perspectives on the self's motives, thoughts, and feelings" (p. 138). When this occurs, social interaction ceases to be a matter of two isolated individuals expressing private thoughts. It now consists of a pair of persons entering, attempting to produce effects on, and being affected by each other's minds. The resulting enrichment of the quality of the social interaction is enormous.

Second, by virtue of role-taking, new levels of cooperation, compromise, and real argument are reached. So long as children are unable to appreciate each other's viewpoints, their arguments are primarily clashes of assertions ("Put it here." "No, here." "No, here."). In order to gain the benefits of human cooperation, a common ground must be reached. A negotiation process, designed to reconcile and adjust these different viewpoints, must come into play. By entering the other's mind, compromise becomes possible, ultimately redounding to the mutual benefit of both persons.

Third, role-taking makes possible a level of human closeness and intimacy that would be inconceivable in its absence. For example, one can perceive a radical difference between the bonds that attach young children and those that attach adolescents to other people. The young child can feel profound love for someone, but it is not a love that is deepened and enriched by interpersonal understanding. Children's love for parents is largely based on the satisfactions that parents provide. Children's fondness for one another stems from the pleasure that each gives to the other.

Adolescent friendship, of course, also depends on mutual pleasure; but, in addition, it involves a feeling of closeness and intimacy that can only come from mutual understanding, from the sharing of one another's inner worlds (Jourard 1964). When people are able to get inside one another's minds, these minds are in a sense joined. Other people's thoughts become part of one's own mental content.

One can observe this difference when comparing the bases of friendship among children and among adolescents. To the young child, friendship exists on a "physicalistic and literal basis" (Selman, 1980, p. 136). A friend is someone who plays with the child and likes to do the same things. As young people mature, however, they come to believe that friendship depends largely on the exchange and sharing of mental events: "Each person is seen as capable of taking into account the other's perspectives on the self's motives, thoughts, and feelings" (p. 138). At the more advanced stage of friendship,

> "closeness within friendship . . . is seen in the degree to which two persons share intimate personal concerns and the effort they make to maintain the relationship. Trust is a major conceptual force in the vocabulary of subjects whose understanding is coded at this stage; it signifies that each party is willing to share these intimate thoughts and feelings with his or her partner, thoughts and feelings that are not shared with less intimate friends and acquaintances." (Selman 1980, p. 140)

It is clear from these observations that the *depth* of human understanding can be greatly increased as a result of role-taking.

Equally important to human beings is the fact that, as a result of role-taking, the child's intellectual powers are greatly strengthened and broadened. When people are able to enter one another's minds, intellectual horizons expand, a broader understanding is achieved, and logical processes come into operation. People's minds, feeding on the different perspectives and ideas of other human beings, grow, expand, and flourish. No longer exclusively locked into their idiosyncratic viewpoints, role-takers gain a broader and deeper understanding of the world and of people.

Control

Having discovered that people have minds, children gradually come to recognize that their own interests can best be served by producing intended effects on those minds. In time they make the world-shaking discovery that the ability to affect others' minds is the most effective way of determining other people's behavior.

In the early years, the reasons for wanting to produce effects on others' minds are apt to be largely self-interested. We want a friend to join us in a game, an adult to give us candy, a mother to stop shouting at us, a sibling to lend us a bicycle. In later years, too, self-interested motives continue to play a prominent role. Our attempts to alter the contents of someone's mind may include inducing a customer to purchase our product; getting someone to love us; getting people to provide us with comfort, sympathy, and support; and so on. In adulthood, however, many non–self-interested motives also underlie people's thought-control efforts. The adult may be more concerned with the welfare of the listener or with some abstract cause than with the self. To help out a friend, I may attempt to persuade an employer to hire him. Or I may seek to convince a legislator to vote a certain way in order to protect the environment. But whether people work to advance their own or others' interests, the method is the same—to produce intended effects on the minds of others.

Intended effects, of course, do not necessarily have a benign purpose. A person may be just as interested in misleading as in enlightening the listener. For example, in Shakespeare's *Othello*, Iago plants doubts about Desdemona's fidelity in Othello's mind in order to bring about the downfall of the Moor. Another, less damaging, illustration of such interpersonal manipulation is the classic episode of the whitewashed fence in Mark Twain's *The Adventures of Tom Sawyer*. Aunt Polly, it will be recalled, had told Tom to whitewash the fence, a task he loathed. As his friends passed by, he convinced them that whitewashing the fence was a privilege rather than a chore. Soon the boys were pleading with Tom to allow them to whitewash the fence. He reluctantly acceded to their request, at the same time extracting payment from them for conferring on them this great benefit.

Stories of confidence men also exemplify the manipulation process. In the confidence game, the mark is eventually bilked of his money without ever knowing that he has been cheated. The confidence man begins with one fundamental role-taking assumption—that everyone has larceny in his heart and is eager to make some easy money. If this assumption is wrong, the entire operation fails. After that, an elaborate scenario is acted out keeping in mind the mark's perception of the situation.

The benefits of role-taking, then, are both wide-ranging and profound. It greatly improves the prediction of others' behavior, thereby contributing to the establishment of a more stable, secure world; it makes baffling events comprehensible, converting meaningless facts into meaningful ones; it makes possible communication—the sharing of mental events—without which social life would be impossible and the human being would not be truly human; it brings depth and richness to interpersonal relationships, the most precious of human experiences; and, since most of what we want out of life depends on other people, it makes possible the fulfillment of human needs and desires by enabling us to affect other people's thoughts and feelings in certain ways. It would seem to be almost impossible to overestimate the importance of role-taking in people's lives.

Expressive and Instrumental Speech

Although words are the most obvious way of producing intended effects on others' minds, they are not the only way. For one thing, children learn that they can affect others' thoughts by their own behavior. Getting answers right in school does more to convince others that they are smart than a thousand boastful words. They also learn that they can affect another person's thoughts by means of nonverbal gestures: choosing a certain facial expression (smiling, frowning, looking irritable); speaking in a certain tone of voice (forcefully or timidly, enthusiastically or dispassionately); dressing in a certain way (conservatively or boldly); or making use of various props or settings. Finally, they learn that they can affect other people's thoughts by exposing them to selected stimuli. They may thrust their report cards before their parents' eyes if the results are good but conceal them if they are bad.

Nevertheless, the best way to produce intended effects on others' minds is to use words—or, as Mead (1934) expressed it, "verbal gestures." Effective speech—that is, speech designed to produce intended effects on minds (and thereby on behavior)—depends on taking the role of the other. This becomes particularly apparent when we consider the distinction between expressive and instrumental speech.

Among adults, I believe, most speech is instrumental, that is, purposive. When grown-ups speak, they usually do so in order to produce intended effects on their listeners' minds. The kinds of effects they may wish to produce are, of course, well-nigh endless. They may wish to inform, to enlighten, to amuse, to convince, to frighten, to activate, to excite, to calm, to confuse, to mislead, to distract, to insult, or to produce any of an enormous number of general and specific effects on other people's minds.

In instrumental speech, then, attention is focused on the internal mental events of the listener. Although I may speak partly to get something off my mind (expressive speech), more often I want to produce a certain effect on yours (instrumental speech). Were I not concerned with the effect of my words on your mind, I could just as well speak with no one else present (as young children often do). True, I may gain some comfort from telling my troubles to my dog, who is invariably a sympathetic listener, but that is usually a poor substitute for the real thing. Adults also speak for expressive reasons (for example, to ventilate their feelings); but in general, adults speak to produce some effect on another person's mind. Instrumental speech is thus role-taking speech. Instrumental speech serves as a means to an end. Expressive speech (non–role-taking speech), on the other hand, is an end in itself. It is not intended to produce an impact on the mind of the listener but to verbalize the thoughts that cross the speaker's mind.

Developmental Processes

When young children speak, they are largely indifferent to their listeners' internal mental events. Hence, their speech tends to be expressive rather than instrumental.

Consider some of the children's conversations recorded by Piaget (1932, pp. 57–58):

Pie: "Where can we make another tunnel? Ah, here Eun?"
Eun: "Look at my pretty frock."
Cat: "Have you finished, Bur?"
Bur: "Now it goes that way again."
Den to Geo in the building room: "I know how to, you'll see how well I know. You don't know how." (No answer. Den then goes back to her place.) "I know how."

The following, which appears to be a conversation, is, as Piaget correctly notes, more appropriately described as a "collective monologue."

Lev: "It all begins with Goldylocks. I'm writing the story of the three bears. The daddy bear is dead. Only the daddy was too ill."
Gen: "I used to live at Saleve. I lived in a little house and you had to take the funicular railway to go and buy things."
Geo: "I can't do the bear."
Li: "That's not Goldylocks."
Lev: "I haven't got curls."

A noteworthy feature of these conversations is the speaker's indifference to the irrelevance of the other person's responses. Often a child asks a question and is totally unconcerned with the fact that they receive no answer. Children speak simply for the pleasure of talking, not for the purpose of communicating—"not unlike a certain type of drawing-room conversation where everyone talks about himself and no one listens" (Piaget 1932, p. 9).

Our interpretations of instrumental speech and expressive speech are thus radically different. For example, assume that a man makes certain self-deprecatory remarks about his ability to do something. Viewing these words as expressive, we interpret them as reflections of his negative opinion of himself. But if we view these words as instrumental, we may conclude that he is "fishing for compliments." By speaking negatively of himself, he anticipates that others, governed by the norms of politeness, will contradict him. People may thus publicly and unwarrantedly derogate themselves in order to undergo the delightful experience of hearing themselves praised to the skies.

Similarly, when people look sad and tell us their tales of woe, we may interpret these words as an expression of their inner feelings of sorrow. In fact, however, the purpose of the words may be to elicit our sympathy, to get us to lend them money, to induce us to assume their burdens, and so on. In interpreting adult speech, then, we must ask what the speaker is trying to accomplish.

Whereas in expressive speech we may be unconcerned with its effects on others, instrumental speech is squarely oriented toward the thoughts and feelings of the listener. As a result, people can construct messages that are far more effective in producing intended effects on others' thoughts and behaviors. Flavell's (1968) comparisons of children's and adolescents' messages aptly illustrate this point. In this investigation, subjects of different ages were asked to indicate how they would go about persuading their fathers to buy them a television set for their rooms (pp. 136, 144–45). Children in grades 3, 7, and 11 were given the following instructions:

> Now suppose that you wanted a TV set for your own room real *bad,* and you are trying to get your father to buy one for you. . . . You'll try to use *every* argument you can think of which might talk him into buying it for you. . . . Go ahead and try to talk him into it.

Third grader's message:
Come on, I want a television for my own room. Come on. Please, Daddy, come on. Buy me a television. I want one for my room. Come on. Come on, Daddy. I want you to. There!

Seventh grader's message:
Say, Dad, a lot of kids at school I know are getting televisions for Christmas. Can I have one? Gee, I know a lot of kids that want one, gee. I could really use it, you—for some of the educational programs, you know, that are on TV, and they're real good, and for homework at night some of our teachers want [us] to watch 'em, and—you know, Johnnie always wants to watch cowboys, and . . . and everything, and I—I'll never get a chance to watch it down there, so why can't I have it in my room? C'mon Dad, please.

Eleventh grader's message:
Dad, ah . . . it gets pretty lonely up there in my room at times, and—it'd be very nice if I could have a companion. . . . I'd like to have—well, maybe a very small TV set. . . . But it doesn't cost that much, I mean. After all, I could use some of my allowance to pay for it. . . . I could—I could get

a job even—'cause I really want that TV set. . . . I'll even clean up my room every day. I'll make my own bed in the morning. . . . Well, I know I should make my bed, but—I want that TV set and I'll—I'll make everybody's bed in the morning if I can have that TV set. . . . There's lots of things I have to watch on TV for school, and . . . I don't get a chance to see much educational ones. . . . No, I won't listen to (popular program) all the time, I'll listen to educational ones, too.

These examples clearly reveal the degree to which thought-control depends on thought-reading. In formulating the message, the more mature speaker carefully considers the listener's interests, attitudes, values, etc. First, the speaker, looking into the listener's mind, makes the assumption that the father values successful academic performance. Hence, the reference by both the seventh and eleventh graders to the educational value of TV or its relevance for school. Second, the older child imputes to the father a concern with costs, and seeks to meet this concern by providing some of the money from her allowance. Third, the speaker seeks to deal in advance with some of the anticipated counterarguments—denying that the set will be used to watch a popular teenage show and assuring the father that it will be used for more praiseworthy purposes. It is also worth noting that one of the father's mental events that the adolescent considers is the father's anticipated efforts to grasp the adolescent's mental events. For example, the adolescent anticipates that the father may attribute to her certain ulterior motives, and takes account of these in formulating her message. Fourth, the older child offers to negotiate, anticipating that the father may set forth certain conditions and proposing a counteroffer. The quid pro quo she offers is to make her bed. Once the argument is verbalized, however, she immediately recognizes its weakness, namely, that it is her responsibility to make her bed anyway. Hence, a new offer is made—to make everyone's bed.

As children mature, the nature of their message-fashioning is radically altered. In the third grade messages are still primitive and show little effort at thought-reading. The young child appears to have little insight into the father's mind, little ability to anticipate the father's response to his message. At this stage, the child is not able to move far beyond the level of pleas and threats. Among older children, in contrast, the message is decidedly distinct from the thought that initiated it. Note that the adolescent does not say that she wants the TV set for her own pleasure. Rather, the arguments are posed in terms of the educational advantages of the TV set (hardly likely to be the speaker's central objective), issues of cost, considerations of fairness (all the other kids have one), offers for negotiation (to contribute one's own money, to make everyone's bed), anticipated objections (that the set would be used for a less worthy purpose), and so on.

Instrumental and Expressive Differences

In sum, it is apparent that instrumental (socialized) speech, involving the tailoring of messages to the mental events of the listener, differs from expressive (egocentric) speech in a number of ways. I would like to call attention to five of these.

1. Instrumental speech is not an end in itself but a means to an end. The end is to produce effects on the other's mind, often for the purpose of producing desired alterations in the listener's behavior.

2. Instrumental speech depends heavily on thought-reading. The message constructed is based largely on the speaker's assumptions about the listener's interests, attitudes, values, and motives. The speaker is actively engaged in rummaging around the listener's mind, seeking to discover what is there in order to construct the most effective message.

3. Instrumental speech involves the anticipation of the response of the listener to one's message. The child who anticipates that the father will challenge the necessity for the purchase (why can't the child watch the set in the living room?) will explain that such a solution conflicts with the needs of other family members—clearly a noble and altruistic concern.

4. The construction of the message involves a complex process of reacting to one's own statement from the viewpoint of the listener. Thus the girl who offers to make her bed if she is given a television set recognizes (and recognizes that her father recognizes) that she is expected to make her bed anyway. Hence, in the spirit of negotiation, she revises her message with an offer to make everyone's bed.

5. A verbal statement can, and often does, reflect multiple motives or intentions. Although one reason for telling you about some historical event is to provide you with knowledge that you lack, an ulterior reason may be to impress you with my intelligence; or, if my intent is more hostile, to humiliate you by revealing your ignorance. When I tell someone a nasty joke about a mutual acquaintance, I may be trying to amuse the listener and at the same time induce in him or her a negative attitude toward the butt of the joke. It is thus not always easy to identify the specific purpose that underlies speech. But the general purpose is clear—to produce intended effects on the mind of the other.

In instrumental speech, the message that is finally verbalized reflects the thoughts that are concealed as well as the thoughts that are revealed. The inhibition of a hostile thought is as much a part of the message-fashioning process as the words designed to have a direct impact. For example, assume that in the course of conversation there pops into my head a joke involving some sickness. As I struggle to formulate the message in the most amusing way, I suddenly remember that the listener's spouse suffers from the disease. Taking the role of the other, I anticipate that the listener will respond negatively to my joke. I therefore suppress the thought. The point is that what I do not say is as much a part of the message-fashioning process as what I do say.

It is thus apparent that, among more mature minds, a message is not simply the spontaneous ventilation of internal thoughts and feelings. On the contrary, it is a carefully constructed product. The commonsense idea that when people speak they are saying what is on their minds (expressive speech) is a misconception. A thought is only a stimulus for the construction of a message. The message itself is a creative construction which may include, *among other elements,* the initiating thought.

Although the intentional effort to control the other person's cognitive content is most clearly evident in the process of persuasion, I believe that the same process operates, although sometimes less explicitly, when other thought-control objectives are involved. Given the complexity of the process and the multiplicity of purposes it serves, it is no wonder that the full development of this ability does not appear until later childhood or adolescence.

Normative Influences

Messages are heavily influenced by cultural norms, not in the simple sense of language, but in the sense that societies do or do not accord legitimacy to the reasons offered for behavior. For example, it may be legitimate for me to hurt someone in self-defense, but not for the purpose of robbery. It may be legitimate for me to lie in the interests of patriotism or loyalty to friends or family, but not to exploit people (see Kohlberg 1976). In other words, reasons for behavior that may be acceptable in one society (or societal subgroup) may not be acceptable in another. Hence, in fashioning messages, people may utilize what Mills (1940) once referred to as "vocabularies of motives" that lay claim to legitimacy and that listeners are under social obligation to accept (see also Scott and Lyman 1968).

When adults speak, then, their intention is not simply to express what is on their minds. Rather, a message is formulated in the silence of one's mind, and the speaker reflects on how the words will sound to the listener, that is, how the listener, given his or her interests, attitudes, values, and beliefs, is likely to respond to the message. On the basis of these role-taking inferences, the speaker may modify the message in a fashion better designed to produce the intended effect (or to avoid an undesired effect). This process is vividly illustrated in the phenomenon of "disclaimers." The chief purpose of disclaimers, Hewitt and Stokes (1975) point out, is to ward off or forestall negative typifications of us that our words may arouse. Hewitt and Stokes have identified five types of disclaimers.

Hedging. One purpose of hedging is to allow one to retreat readily if one's statement is challenged or contradicted. It is reflected in such prefaces as "I'm no expert, of course, but . . ." "I could be wrong in my facts, but I think . . ." "I really haven't thought this through very well, but . . ." Anticipating that the listener may have an opposing view, one hedges one's statement in order to make it easier to retreat from a position without loss of face and without the need to argue in favor of an indefensible position.

Credentialing. Another device people use is to assert in advance that they anticipate opposition to their ideas and to explain that they are not as discrediting as they may appear to be. For example: "I know what I am going to say seems anthropomorphic, but . . ." "I'm not prejudiced—some of my best friends are Jews—but . . ." "Don't get me wrong, I like your work, but . . ." The aim of such disclaimers is to mitigate or forestall the negative response to the statement that one plans to make.

Sin Licenses. Sin licenses are employed when speakers anticipate that listeners will interpret what they plan to say or do as moral failings. They show that they are aware that they are violating a social rule but that there are extenuating circumstances. They thus show themselves to be responsible and moral members of society despite the deviance. Examples are: "I know you might think this is the wrong thing to do, but . . ." "I know this is against the rules, but . . ." "What I'm going to do is contrary to the letter of the law but not its spirit . . ."

Cognitive Disclaimers. As speakers anticipate possible responses, they may realize that the listener may find their statements incomprehensible. Eager to avoid a negative reaction, speakers may preface their statements with such disclaimers as "This may sound strange to you . . ." "Don't react right away to what I'm going to do . . ." "I know this sounds crazy but I think I saw . . ." The speaker's acknowledgment that the statement about to be made sounds peculiar forestalls the listener's impression that it is, in fact, peculiar.

Appeals for Suspension of Judgment. Speakers may anticipate that the immediate response of the listener to a statement they propose to make will be negative. In order to delay such responses until they have had the opportunity to make the statement more palatable, they begin by asking the listener to suspend judgment temporarily: "I don't want to make you angry by saying this, but . . ." "Don't get me wrong, but . . ." "Hear me out before you explode . . ."

The use of disclaimers vividly illustrates the fact that the speaker, *before* verbalizing the message, takes account of the listener's anticipated reaction to it. Anticipating that the other person will treat something I am planning

to say as a double entendre (which would defeat my thought-control intention), I choose an alternative innocuous way of expressing the same idea.
Thinking that a certain phrase will sound mealy-mouthed to the listener's
ears, I search for a more direct and forceful way of expressing it. Recogniz-
ing that the listener may be ignorant of some term I propose to use, I preface
my statement with an explanation of its meaning.

The speech act, then, is a multistaged process which demands simultaneous attention to two minds: ego's and alter's. When a message is fashioned, it is not necessarily verbalized instantly. Frequently it is first re-
viewed, and its probable impact on the other's mind assessed in the light of
certain inferences regarding the other's psychological interior. As a result of
this internal process, the message may be edited, revised, or reconstructed
in various ways. Its expression may be silently rehearsed and, on that basis,
further edited, reformulated, and improved. Clearly, this is an extremely
complex process and includes as a central feature the constant effort to read
the thoughts of the other.

One difference between expressive and instrumental speech, then, is
that in expressive speech the initiating thought and the spoken statement
tend to be the same, whereas in instrumental speech the two are likely to
differ, often very sharply. In instrumental speech, spoken statements rest
upon assumptions about the contents of others' minds. I do not speak to
people in a language that I assume they do not understand. I do not address
a child as I do an adult. The topics I discuss with a cab driver differ from
those that I discuss with my wife. I do not ask a citizen of Tibet who will
win the World Series. I do not express condolences to someone who has
just won the lottery. I do not congratulate someone who has just suffered
a personal tragedy. When I communicate, then, I adjust my message to the
assumed knowledge, interests, attitudes, values, and motives of the listener.
The question is; How do people go about exploring the thoughts and feelings of other people?

Role-Taking Processes

To know what others are thinking is of major importance to human beings,
yet few things are more difficult to do. There are several reasons why this
is so. The first is that there is simply no way to evade the unalterable and
inescapable fact that, in the final analysis, every human being is encapsu-
lated in his or her own phenomenal world. Direct access to the mind of any
other human being is forever barred to us. Second, other people are often
motivated to draw the veil around their inner thoughts and feelings. They
use a variety of devices to confuse or mislead us, to keep us in the dark
about those internal events. And they can do so precisely because they are
able to take our roles.

Even if we know someone extremely well, it is often difficult to enter the inner sanctum of their minds. How much more difficult it must be, then, to ascertain the thoughts of people we have never even seen? At the market I must deal with a checkout clerk who is a complete stranger to me (as I as to him or her). At the beginning of a semester I must make a wide-ranging series of assumptions about the informational content, intentions, motives, and values of a large number of students whom I have never met.

Inferences

What do socialized actors do in the face of this problem? They make *inferences*. To quote Flavell (1968, p. 209): "Role-taking activity is an inferential process . . . a process of making guesses . . ."

How do people make such inferences? One way is to observe how others act. When we see someone kissing and hugging a child, we infer the presence of an underlying feeling of love. When we see one person hitting another on the jaw, we infer the existence of an underlying feeling of hostility. When we see one person greeting another effusively, we infer friendly feelings. And so on. People may place greater confidence in inferences based on people's behavior than on their words.

Inferences about others' mental events are also made on the basis of learned patterns of person perception (Tagiuri 1969). Given a specific item of information, people may attribute a number of other characteristics. For example, an important basis for inferring internal mental events is the individual's social identity elements, that is, his or her socially recognized groups, statuses, or social categories. Although sociologists usually focus on the behavioral expectations associated with these identity elements, I suggest that a complex system of cognitive expectations are also attached to them. Knowing a person's social position not only enables us to predict how he or she will act; it also enables us to predict how he or she will think.

Many kinds of thoughts and feelings (some described earlier) are imputed to people by virtue of their social roles. One is the simple matter of knowledge. We assume that doctors have *knowledge* of certain medical facts, psychologists of psychological concepts, and so on. Second, we impute to role incumbents certain *interests*. We assume that men are more interested in sports than women; that adults are more concerned about business than children; that builders are more interested in zoning regulations than nonbuilders; and so on. Third are *emotions*. We assume that a mother loves her children, that a prima donna is temperamental, that an accountant is coldly analytical. Fourth are *beliefs, opinions, and attitudes*. We assume that stock brokers are politically conservative, that Ku Klux Klaners are prejudiced, that journalists believe in press freedom. Fifth are *values*. We assume that judges value justice, that ministers value morality, that environmentalists value the protection of nature. Sixth are *motives*.

We assume that an entrepreneur's actions are motivated by a desire for profit, that a chess champion is motivated by the desire for victory. Knowing nothing more than a person's social identity, people read a volume of information about the inner contents of that person's mind, despite the fact that all they are seeing is the cover.

Stereotypical inferences are also based on physical characteristics and traits. For example, people draw inferences about others' internal characteristics on the basis of how they look. Studies show that when subjects are presented with pictures of men with dark complexions and coarse oily skins, they infer that these people are hostile, quick-tempered, sly, and unpleasant (Secord, Dukes, and Bevan 1954). Pictures of people wearing glasses tend to produce the inference that they are more intelligent and less humorous than others (Livesley and Bromley 1973).

Stereotypical thought also applies to traits. Probably the key finding in the literature on person perception is the fact that if people know one thing about a person, they characteristically draw inferences about a number of others. For example, people told that a man is *warm* are much more likely than those told that he is *cold* to describe him as generous and humorous (Asch 1946).

Finally, of course, people draw inferences about others' internal mental events on the basis of prior experience. If we know a person well, our inferences will differ from those we make about people we hardly know.

Human beings, then, do not enter an interactional situation devoid of assumptions about the contents of others' minds. On the contrary, we bring to social interaction a vast fund of preconceptions. Without them, we cannot even begin to interact successfully with others. But our assumptions are often in error. The football player we are chatting with turns out to have a fondness for knitting. The professor, assumed to be intelligent and knowledgeable, proves to be an ignoramus. Although stereotypical assumptions about people's cognitive contents are often wrong, people depend on them, at least provisionally, because they have nothing else to go on. In the absence of such assumptions, they are at a loss about what to say or how to say it.

Thought-reading, then, is a complex inferential process. Assumptions about others are held tentatively, subject to revision in the light of new information. But whether these inferences are sure or uncertain, they are the essential foundation upon which all social interaction rests.

Role-Taking and Mental Disorder

The effort to penetrate the mystery of other people's inner worlds is thus a continuing activity of human adults. We are constantly probing other people's thoughts and feelings, making assumptions about what they know, want, intend, believe, feel, value, and so on. For the socialized mind, thought-reading is a constant ongoing feature of social life.

What happens, however, when people are *not* able to take the role of the other? They find themselves unable to grasp the actor's viewpoint. They cannot place themselves in the actor's shoes, cannot understand the actor's internal world. When this occurs, an insuperable barrier is erected between human beings. When we have no idea why someone sits on a hospital bench staring at the wall for hours on end; eats soup with a fork and meat with a spoon; believes the television announcer is making fun of him—when these things happen, the most fundamental rupture in human relations occurs. The human bond is snapped. The inability to take the role of the other thus produces a profound separation of people from one another, a separation more complete than that imposed by physical distance, personal enmity, or even death.

The central argument of this book can now be stated. The defining feature of mental disorder, I suggest, is the fact that the observer is unable to take the role of the actor. This generalization, however, is subject to two important qualifications. The first deals with the process of causal attribution, the second with socially shared belief systems.

Causal Attributions

In studying the naive actor's explanation of the causes of outcomes, attribution theorists have distinguished those causes that are viewed as internal (e.g., ability or effort) and those that are viewed as external (e.g., chance, luck, or other environmental factors) (Heider 1958; Kelley 1967; Weiner et al. 1971). For example, if someone does well on a test, the explanation may be that the individual is intelligent (internal cause) or that the test was easy (external cause).

With respect to the attribution of mental disorder, it is crucial that we understand the cause of the role-taking failure. If I find myself unable to take the role of the other, I may attribute this thought-reading failure either to myself (there is something about me that prevents me from understanding the other person) or to the other (there is something about that person that makes him or her incomprehensible). I suggest that if the role-taking failure is internal—if we believe that our inability to understand the other person is attributable to our own limitations—then we suspend judgment about the mental status of the TEB. If, on the other hand, the role-taking failure is viewed as external (the other person is incomprehensible to ourselves or, we assume, to society at large), then we consider the possibility that the person is mentally disordered.

Under what circumstances are people likely to attribute this role-taking failure to themselves rather than to the other person? At least five can be specified.

The first is a situation in which the other person's *cognitive structure* is of such a radically different order that we abandon hope of ever being able to fathom it. This is likely to occur, for example, if the other is in the precommunicative stage. A familiar illustration is our response to the behavior of infants and babies. However much we strive to enter the minds of babies, their actions are often experienced as unfathomable. We are at a loss to understand why the baby is howling at the top of its lungs or is clinging so frantically to some ragged shred of blanket. Indeed, there is a sense in which every parent finds his or her infant's behavior to have a lunatic quality. Nevertheless, babies are not considered mentally disordered; the parents simply feel that they lack both the acumen and the necessary information to understand the infant's viewpoint. This also explains why the behavior of animals, though also incomprehensible to us, is not considered mentally disordered.

Another insuperable barrier to interpersonal understanding is ignorance of the other person's *language*. If we do not know the meaning of the other person's words, we are at a loss to understand their internal mental events. Even though we cannot grasp the other's point of view, however, we assume that it is our own ignorance, not the actor's mental disorder, that is the cause of its incomprehensibility.

The fault for role-taking failure is also assigned to ourselves when we are unable to understand the behavior of members of an alien *culture*. The behavior of the African shaman, the Indian yogi, or the religious charismatic, although perhaps beyond our understanding, is not judged to be mentally disorder. We recognize that in order to understand behavior, we need to know a culture's ways of thought, such as its systems of logic, assumptions about reality, major motives, values, life interests, and so on. Realizing that we have not been socialized to understand these ways of thought, we attribute our failure to understand the actor's viewpoint to our own lack of knowledge, not to the actor's mental disorder.

We also recognize that other people's worlds of experience may be so specialized and remote from our own that we attribute our failure to understand their viewpoints to our own *lack of knowledge*. Many people within our own society say and do things that we find incomprehensible. Lawyers use words in ways that dumbfound us; doctors, for reasons beyond our understanding, shine lights in our eyes, apply pressure to portions of our anatomy, draw blood from our veins; mathematicians scrawl strange squiggles on paper; and so on. Though all this is mysterious to us, we attribute our failure to understand their words and their actions to our own intellectual limitations.

We also attribute role-taking failure to ourselves when we realize that we are ignorant of the context in which the TEB appears. For example, the specific act of sliding into second base is only meaningful when viewed within the context of the baseball game. People therefore recognize that the inability to take the role of the other may be caused by an inadequate understanding of the context. For example, if we enter a room and find a number of people moving their arms, legs, and torsos wildly about, we are apt to find such behavior incomprehensible. But when we learn that we have come upon an exercise class (or, perhaps, a dance), we are provided with sufficient information about the context to understand the behavior. Similarly, when we see a man pacing back and forth hour after hour, we may think that we are witnessing a severe compulsion or state of psychomotor agitation. This senseless behavior becomes comprehensible, however, when we discover that this is a soldier guarding an entrance.

Whether we attribute role-taking failure to ourselves or to the other may depend on the connection between our social position and that of the person with whom we are interacting. Consider, for example, the network of role relationships that connects members of society, with each role linked to others through a given "role-set" (Merton 1957). Other things being equal, we would expect the following:

1. People occupying the same statuses will more easily grasp one another's perspectives than those occupying different statuses. For example, a college student can more easily understand another student's viewpoint than the viewpoint of a professor, university administrator, or government official.

2. People can more successfully adopt the perspective of those in their own role-set than that of those in a different role-set. Professors can more readily understand the perspectives of students, university administrators, or other professors than they can those of physicians, nurses, or hospital administrators.

3. The more remote the role connection, the less likely are people to understand one another's perspectives. The lumberjack will have difficulty understanding the architect's perspective, and the architect will have difficulty comprehending the fisherman's point of view.

In addition to these structural bases of interpretive diversity, cultural and interpersonal factors affect our role-taking ability. We grasp the viewpoint of members of our own culture or subculture more readily than we do those of a different one. Second, we are likely to better understand the perspective of those with whom we interact frequently than that of those with whom we have little contact. Finally, failure to understand the other's viewpoint may stem from ignorance of many other relevant facts. These facts may be historical or biographical in nature—facts which we cannot reasonably be expected to know.

In sum, the idea that the defining feature of mental disorder is unsuccessful role-taking is subject to an important qualification: if observers attribute this failure to their own limitations, then they suspend judgment about the mental status of the act. They may not consider these thoughts to be sane, in a positive sense, but neither do they conclude that they are mentally disordered. The tendency is to take no position on the issue. It is only when they assign the blame for their role-taking failure to the other person that they may call into question his or her mental status.

Subcultural Belief Systems

A second qualification to the role-taking theory of insanity is the following: if a TEB is an element of a socially shared belief system, then it is not considered to be mentally ill. For example, suppose we are told that a socially and academically successful college student from a stable middle-class family has dropped out of school, shaved his head, donned a bright orange robe, and taken to dancing around congested city streets repeatedly chanting nonsense syllables. We would not long hesitate to conclude that he has become mentally ill. But when we are told that this young man has become a member of the Hare Krishna sect, our attitude toward him changes. Although we do not understand this behavior any better, we nevertheless do not consider it insane.

Why not? The reason is that this behavior is part of a socially shared belief system. If this young man were alone in displaying this behavior, he would almost certainly be judged insane. But if a group shares this belief system or engages in shared behavioral practices, then the sanity of the behavior is not challenged. To be sure, many an observer seeing a group of Hare Krishna followers chanting and dancing in the streets may think "they're all crazy," but this judgment is not meant literally.

It is thus not surprising that DSM–III–R explicitly exempts shared behavioral practices or belief systems from its classification of mental disorders. According to DSM–III–R (p. 193): "Beliefs or experiences of members of religious or other cultural groups may be difficult to distinguish from delusions or hallucinations. When such experiences are shared and accepted by a cultural group, they should not be considered evidence of psychosis."

The central argument of this work can now be put in a nutshell: When people find that they are unable to take the role of the other, they may come to characterize the thought, emotion, or behavior as mentally ill. The only exceptions to this generalization are if they attribute the role-taking failure to their own limitations and if they recognize the TEB as an element in a socially shared belief system. Mental illness, in this view, is an interpersonal phenomenon; it represents a failure in interpersonal understanding.

3
Incomprehensible Thoughts, Emotions, and Behaviors

T he central argument of this book is that, despite the enormous range and variation of mentally disordered TEBs, they all have one feature in common, namely, that other people find them incomprehensible. But what kind of TEBs tend to defy people's role-taking efforts? That is the question addressed in this chapter.

Before attempting to describe these insane TEBs, however, there are two prior issues that must be considered. The first deals with the issue of professional diagnosis, the second, with the issue of social consensus.

Lay and Professional Interpretations

In arguing that role-taking failure determines whether thought, emotion, or behavior is insane, I am not suggesting that professional diagnoses rest on this foundation. Professionals take into account many factors in making diagnostic decisions: the presence or absence of specific signs or symptoms, deterioration from a previous level of functioning, age of onset, duration of disorder, nature of impairment, family history, and much more. Professional diagnoses, then, do not rest on role-taking failure; rather, they are based on the correspondence between observed behavior and certain specified criteria that are currently incorporated into authoritative diagnostic manuals. It may seem, then, that role-taking theory is irrelevant to professional diagnosis.

If we probe more deeply, however, we see that the roots of professional diagnosis itself can be traced to role-taking failure. Consider the question; How does a person become a mental patient? Mechanic (1962, pp. 67) notes: "The early definitions of mental illness, especially in middle-class populations, are likely to take place in the groups within which the person primarily operates: evaluations are made by family, fellow employees, friends, and employers." In the lower class, the community agency, the police, and the courts are apt to play a more important role. But in either case, it is basically society—or the individual her or himself—that brings the individual to the attention of the psychiatric professional. According to

Mechanic (1962, p. 69); "The basic decision about [mental] illness is usually made by community members and not professional personnel."

In other words, the person who is brought to the professional's attention in the first place has displayed a thought, emotion, or behavior that is incomprehensible to the layperson. And the professional will usually conclude that the person brought to his or her attention because of psychiatric problems is indeed mentally ill. Reporting on his research in the sixties, Mechanic says that he never saw a person turned away at a mental hospital because the professional diagnostician judged him or her to be normal. Scheff's (1975, pp. 16–17) studies of commitment proceedings agree with Mechanic's observations. He notes:

> The separation of the members of society along the axis of sanity and insanity is largely a product of social rather than medical or scientific selection. Virtually all persons who are proposed by members of the community (or public agencies such as the police) are accepted for treatment. The medical "examinations" that supposedly determine whether the candidate is sane or insane are, as a rule, peremptory and ritualistic. The actual goal of most of these examinations . . . seems not to be *whether* the candidate is mentally ill but *which* mental illness he has.

Scheff (1984, p. 96) reported that in 196 out of 196 cases, examiners recommended psychiatric treatment.

Because of recent changes in psychiatric practice, such automatic commitment to a mental hospital no longer takes place. But that does not alter the fact that the decision to bring people to the professional's attention in the first place is made by laypersons. In other words, it is laypersons, not professionals, who make the initial diagnosis of mental illness. If we are to understand the nature of insanity, then, we must focus on the layperson's response to people's thoughts, emotions, and behaviors.

The professional's perspective takes up where the layperson's leaves off. He or she assumes that the person brought before him or her is probably mentally disordered. In so doing, he or she implicitly accepts the lay definition of mental disorder. The basic decision about whether someone is or is not mentally disordered, then, is made by *nonprofessionals*. In most cases, this decision is, in effect, accepted by the diagnostician.

The professional's perspective is decidedly different from that of the nonprofessional. Over the course of time many such people are brought to the attention of professionals and certain symptom patterns are observed. Psychiatrists notice that some people who come to their attention are characterized by negative mood, physical lassitude, sleep problems, eating disorders, feelings of guilt, feelings of hopelessness. This syndrome comes to be classified as Major Depression. Other people, they observe, exhibit entirely different reactions. They experience terrible attacks of panic that are often accompanied by sweating, trembling, choking, tingling sensations, heart pounding. People with these symptoms come to be classified as victims of Anxiety Disorders (or one of its subcategories).

In other words, on the basis of cumulative experience, professionals come to discern and identify characteristics common to certain patients and to observe how these symptoms cohere empirically. In time, they classify, formalize, and systematize these symptom patterns or syndromes. As knowledge grows, this information comes to be incorporated into formal diagnostic manuals and to be transmitted to new generations of professionals.

When professionals make their diagnoses, then, they do *not* base their assessments on their inability to take the role of the actor. They do so, rather, by matching the observed symptom patterns of the patients to the templates provided by the official diagnostic manuals.

But this does not conflict with the view that the decisive determinant of mental disorder is role-taking failure. The reason is that, although the psychiatrist is apt to make his or her diagnosis chiefly on the basis of these symptoms, if we trace these symptoms back to their roots, we will find that they arose out of the *layperson's* failure to attribute meaningful cause, intention, motive, or purpose to the actor.

I thus suggest that diagnostic instruments, although they are immediate intellectual property of the trained professional, can be traced back ultimately to the role-taking failure of laypersons. This does not imply that diagnostic instruments are unprofessional or faulty: on the contrary, major impressive advances in diagnosis have been made in recent years, most notably synthesized in DSM–III–R (American Psychiatric Association 1987). What role-taking theory does is to reveal these diagnostic instruments for what they really are: a specification of certain types of thoughts, emotions, and behavior that *most people* in the society find incomprehensible. Otherwise expressed, the behavior that observers are unable to comprehend from the viewpoint of the actor is the same behavior that the psychiatrist comes to classify as mentally disordered. The ultimate decision regarding whether or not a person is mentally ill is thus made by nonprofessionals—by ordinary people who are unable to grasp actor's mental events.

Social Consensus

Role-taking theory views mental disorder as a *dyadic* event—a process involving the interaction between a specific observer and a specific actor. But if this is so, then how is it possible to get beyond the specific dyadic relationship to identify more general (perhaps even universal) characteristics of mental disorder? Unless we are able to do so, the sanity of the actor— or, to be more exact, of the TEB—would have to rest on the idiosyncratic judgment of the particular observer. In other words, if A is able to comprehend someone's viewpoint but B is not, then we would have to conclude that the individual is sane from A's viewpoint but insane from B's. There would be no general basis for deciding whether a person or a TEB is or is not mentally disordered.

That is not our position. Mental disorder is based not on idiosyncratic judgments but on *social consensus*. A person is judged to be mentally disordered whose role *most people* in society are unable to take. (I am grateful to William W. Eaton for directing my attention to this point.) This assumed consensus also underpins each individual judgment of the TEB. When people judge certain TEBs to be insane, they do so not only because they find such TEBs to be incomprehensible but also because they assume that *people generally* would consider them to be incomprehensible. For example, if a wife complains to a friend that her husband sees worms growing out of his moustache (to draw an example from Yarrow et al. 1955), she assumes that the friend would also find this perception to be incomprehensible. Indeed, she assumes that anyone else in the society (including the police, the doctor, the judge) would have the same reaction. An attribution of insanity, then, is not anchored exclusively in a particular individual's thought-reading efforts; it is also rooted in assumptions about other people's role-taking behavior.

Furthermore, if society judges a TEB to be mentally disordered, it does so on the basis of an assumed social consensus. We do not judge a TEB to be disordered if only one person is unable to understand the mental and emotional events underpinning it. It is only disordered if most people, confronted with this stimulus, would also experience such role-taking failure. In any specific instance, of course, only a small number of people will actually be directly involved in the identification of a TEB as disordered, but most or all of these people must share the observer's reactions to it as incomprehensible if the TEB is to be considered mentally disordered.

Insanity, then, is attributed to thoughts, emotions, and behaviors that most people in the society are unable to understand. But what is the nature of these TEBs? That question is the focus of this chapter.

Mentally Ill TEBs

Although it is not possible to consider all of the TEBs that are likely to defy most people's thought-reading efforts, it may be helpful to direct attention to some of the more prominent ones, since these clearly reveal a breakdown in interpersonal understanding.

Without laying claim to exhaustiveness, I suggest that most of the TEBs that defeat people's thought-reading efforts fall into the following categories: belief systems, speech, sensory experiences, emotions, purpose, free will, self and identity, erotic arousal, and interpersonal estrangement. Observers tend to find them incomprehensible and to assume that most other people in society do so as well. These TEBs are of such a nature that people cannot reconcile them with their personal experiences, perceive them in the experiences of other people they know, or reconcile them with the general theories of cognition, motivation, and personality that they have learned in the course of socialization.

Belief Systems

When an individual holds a sustained belief that is contradictory to what almost everyone else thinks and that flies squarely in the face of compelling evidence, he or she is said to be harboring a *delusion*. DSM distinguishes no fewer than twelve different types of delusions. Among the widely recognized delusions are delusions of reference, persecutory delusions, and delusions of grandeur.

Delusions of reference are unwarranted beliefs that events have reference to the individual. For example:

> Everybody is in the street because of him; each gesture of these people has some significance for him; newspaper advertisements refer to him; the storm was made especially for him; the edition of Goethe's works in the hospital library is full of hints at him and has been falsified for his sake.
>
> Gradually, but also quite suddenly, the delusions of reference attain full credibility and certainty. School children run after them; the children chase after the street car whenever the patient is riding in one. It is clear enough that they despise and insult him. . . . Always more and more people give him to understand, by all kinds of signs and allusions, etc., that they know all about these misdeeds of his. Even the newspaper reports contain more or less concealed allusions to him. The minister's sermon is directed at him . . . everywhere there is whispering about him. Wherever he turns, signs and signals point at him. (EB, pp. 133–34)

Persecutory delusions refer to people's convictions that certain persons or groups are after them, hate them, fear them, want to torture them, and so on. The persecutors

> are constantly straining every effort to annihilate or at least torture and frighten the patients. Wherever the patients find themselves they are exposed to these hostile forces, be it that their enemies in person pursue the patient from place to place and hide in the walls, in the next room, in the cellar, in the very air; be it that these hostile forces observe and note his every action and thought by means of . . . electrical instruments and influence him by means of mysterious apparatus and magic. (EB, p. 118)

Grandiose delusions involve an exaggerated sense of one's importance or significance.

The patient has "as much money as there are snow-flakes on the ground." He is going to be King of England. A palace of gold and precious stones is being built for him. The Lord is his only master. He has cured all these poor souls in the hospital. . . . The megalomaniac patients have made marvelous inventions; they are prophets, philosophers, world reformers . . . (EB, pp. 119–20, 231)

Other delusions are those involving thought transfer. These include thought broadcasting (the belief that one's thoughts are being broadcast to the outside world); thought insertion (the belief that thoughts are being placed into one's mind); and thought withdrawal (the belief that thoughts are being withdrawn from one's mind, resulting in a diminished number of thoughts remaining).

These beliefs are mentally disordered because they contradict what everyone else thinks and lack logical or evidential support that others can credit. It is apparent to everyone that the person is not Julius Caesar, nor is he as grand and important as he claims to be, nor is the television announcer making fun of him. Most people find themselves unable to take the role of the actor and take it for granted that others would also be unable to do so as well. Unless the belief system or sensory experience is shared by a group, subculture, or culture, it is judged to mentally disordered. Reality, in this sense, is socially constructed.

Speech

Speech is intended to transmit the mental contents of the speaker's mind to the mind of the listener. When a speaker uses words that convey no information or transmit no ideas, the listener is at a loss to comprehend the speaker's mental events. The listener experiences role-taking failure.

A number of such noncommunicative speech patterns have been identified. One of these is called *loosening of associations*. When people speak, as I noted earlier, they do not simply express the thoughts that enter their heads. Rather, they arrange their ideas in the form of a message, giving due consideration to the listener's information needs, interests, motives, and so on. Taking the role of the other, the speaker realizes that, in order to produce the desired interpersonal effect, the later stages of the argument rest on the foundation that has been established earlier. These thoughts are then arranged with an appropriate beginning, middle, and end to form a coherent message—a message that is understandable to the listener.

When this organization is absent—when the listener cannot discern the thread connecting the speaker's words—he or she is unable to comprehend the speaker's thoughts. The following illustration comes from DSM–III–R (p. 400):

Interviewer: "What did you think of the whole Watergate affair?"
Subject: "You know I didn't tune in on that, I felt so bad about it. But

it seemed to get so murky, and everybody's reports were so negative. Huh, I thought, I don't want any part of this, and I don't care who was in on it, and all I could figure out was Artie had something to do with it. Artie was trying to flush the bathroom toilet of the White House or something. She was trying to do something fairly simple. The tour guests stuck or something. She got blamed because the water overflowed, went down in the basement, down to the kitchen. They had a, they were going to have to repaint and restore the White House room, the enormous living room. And then it was at this reunion they were having. And it's just such a mess and I just thought, well, I'm just going to pretend like I don't even know what's going on. So I came downstairs and 'cause I pretended like I didn't know what was going on, I slipped on the floor of the kitchen, cracking my toe, and when I was teaching some kids how to do some double dives.

Another type of speech that conveys little or no information is called *clanging*. In clanging, words are chosen not for the sense they make but for their sound. For example: "I'm not trying to make noise. I'm trying to make sense. If you can make sense out of nonsense, we'll have fun. I'm trying to make sense out of sense. I'm not making sense (cents) anymore. I have to make dollars" (DSM, p. 393).

There are a number of other categories of thought that also fail to convey information. These include *incoherence* (speech that is incomprehensible because there is a lack of logical connection between the words, the words are used in strange ways, the individual uses partial or incomplete phrases or sentences, and so on); *illogical thinking* ("Example: A patient explained that she gave her family IBM cards, which she punched, in an effort to improve communication with them.") (DSM, p. 399); *poverty of content of speech* (the patient uses words but the words convey no message); *neologisms* (the creation of new words or the use of words in a highly idiosyncratic way); *perseverations* (repeating the same words or phrases pointlessly); and *blocking* (sudden interruption of a train of thought without subsequent return to the topic). All these forms of speech leave the listener baffled, unable to understand what message the speaker is trying to convey, what meaning the words have. In such instances, role-taking efforts suffer complete defeat.

Sensory Experiences

Our senses are our windows on the world. They are the way we make contact with external reality. One of the root assumptions of human thought is that sensory experiences are aroused in response to external physical stimuli. Sensory experiences that occur in the absence of such stimuli are called *hallucinations*. What makes an hallucination so difficult to understand is not so much its actual content as the fact that the observer cannot detect the relevant external stimulus.

All of the senses are subject to hallucinations. The following are especially likely to be found among schizophrenics:

1. *Auditory.* The most common sense distortion is hearing voices. These voices may utter one word or a short sentence, usually a rather nasty one. But voices are not the only sounds reported by schizophrenics. They also hear humming, rattling, thundering, shooting, whispering, and various other sounds.

2. *Olfactory.* Psychotics report smelling everything from heavenly perfumes to poisonous vapors. They may smell roses, onions, rotting garbage, or almost any other odor one can think of.

3. *Tactile.* Psychotics may report a wide variety of tactile sensations. They are being pelted with hail, bitten by scorpions, beaten with sticks, burned by fire.

4. *Gustatory.* Schizophrenics report sweet, sour, or bitter tastes even when not eating. Or the taste experiences they report have no connection with the foods they eat.

5. *Visual.* A visual hallucination is an image that does not exist, whereas an illusion is a misperception of an actual stimulus (for example, a man may look into the mirror and see his face distorted and misshapen). Bleuler cites cases of patients who see everything as red, who see two heads on everyone, who see everything upside down, and so on. Such hallucinations are typically the result of organic disorders.

6. *Somatic.* A somatic hallucination is an experience located inside the body. Patients may have the feeling that snakes are crawling inside them, that their bones have turned liquid, that they have growths in their heads, and so on.

Of course the same external stimulus will not necessarily produce the same sense experience in different people. But when reported experiences have no connection with these external events, then observers find the reports incomprehensible; furthermore, they take it for granted that most other people do too. Again, the sole exception is if these sensory experiences are shared by members of a subculture or culture.

Emotions

Traditionally, the emotions have been thought of as "noncognitive phenomena, among the bodily perturbations"; "involuntary and purely affective states" (Harre 1986, p. 2); or "biologically primitive, instinctive response patterns" (Averill 1980, p. 57). In the minds of most people, emotions are connected with the nonrational or irrational realm of human experience. Yet emotions per se are neither rational nor irrational. The rationality of an emotion depends on its causal connection to external stimulus events or intervening cognitive processes. Indeed, recent social psychological research indicates that the identification of the emotion rests heavily on such assumed causal connections. This means that people are guided by an implicit logic that connects stimulus events or cognitions to emotional experiences (Rosenberg 1990).

Examples of this emotional logic are familiar. If I win the lottery, it is logical for me to be elated. If I make a mistake in public, it is logical for me to be embarrassed. If someone insults me, it is logical for me to be angry. If someone compliments me, it is logical for me to be pleased. Human beings in a society thus learn that there is a logical connection between stimulus event, cognitive processing of the event, and emotional response.

Emotional responses that conform to this logic are comprehensible to people. Emotional responses that violate it are not. Among the latter are inappropriate emotions, blunted emotions, excessive emotions, and labile emotions.

Inappropriate Emotions. Although the term "inappropriate emotions" is usually used to refer to emotions that violate the emotional norms of society, the concept can be conceived more broadly as referring to emotions that are discordant with the observed stimulus events. For example, if I feel depressed at winning the lottery, elated at being insulted, or displeased at being complimented, people are likely to be baffled at the internal mental events that are responsible for such strange responses.

Such inappropriate affect is frequently observed among psychotics. For example:

> The patients are able to react to sad news with cheerfulness or even with laughter. These patients will become sad or even more frequently irritated by events to which others would react with indifference or with pleasure. A mere "how-do-you-do" can upset them. (EB, p. 52)

> A catatonic patient was in great fear of a hallucinated Judas Iscariot who was threatening her with a sword. She cried out that the Judas be driven away, but in between she begged for a piece of chocolate. (EB, p. 43)

The phobias also illustrate the loose connection between the external stimulus and the emotional response. Agoraphobics, for example, are afraid of being in public places from which escape might be difficult or help unavailable. Hence, the agoraphobic may be frightened of crowds, tunnels, bridges, or elevators, or of occupying a seat in the middle of the row in a theater. Social phobics are terrified of situations in which they are objects of people's scrutiny. These people may experience panic when eating in public places or using public lavatories. Simple phobia is a residual category that includes any other phobia.

The problem with such fears is that it is difficult for observers to understand the reasons for them. People cannot understand why anyone should experience absolute terror at walking on a crowded street or dining in a restaurant. In other words, they are unable to perceive any logical connection between the stimulus event and the emotional response.

Blunted Emotions. The blunting or absence of emotions is equally difficult for people to understand. Whatever their actual emotional experiences may be, what these patients display is flat or restricted affect. We find such responses in certain seriously deteriorated cases of schizophrenia.

> Many schizophrenics in the later stages cease to show any affect for years and even decades at a time. They sit about the institutions to which they are confined with expressionless faces, hunched up, the image of indifference. They permit themselves to be dressed and undressed like automatons, to be led from their customary place of inactivity to the mess-hall, and back again without expressing any sign of satisfaction or dissatisfaction. (EB, p. 40)

External events that would universally be expected to produce powerful emotional arousal may produce no response whatever. Bleuler reports cases of schizophrenics watching other patients fighting furiously on the ward or even killing one another without showing any change of facial expression, movement, or other response.

Excessive Emotions. It is not the intensity of an emotion, but the lack of connection between the intensity and the stimulus event that people find perplexing. Bleuler again provides an example:

> We also have to mention the fits of anger, cursing and vilification which are released usually by some external event or experience. These patients may begin to curse, not only if one has said something unpleasant to them, but also after a friendly greeting or even in the very midst of what appears to be a congenial conversation. . . . No matter what one says, they still feel insulted, and only become more angry. (EB, p. 224)

It is not that emotions are intense but that their intensity is out of proportion to the nature of the stimulus event. Major Depression is an example. The depressed individual is sad, hopeless, discouraged, down in the dumps. He or she has lost interest in things, gets no pleasure out of life, lacks energy, lacks sexual drive, experiences constant fatigue. These people are likely to have low self-esteem, to feel guilty and inadequate, perhaps to have suicidal thoughts.

Each of these reactions would be comprehensible, given suitable stimulus events. We can understand, for example, that a person may feel sad at the loss of a loved one, the frustration of a cherished goal, or the report of a serious illness; that he or she should be hopeless or discouraged when life difficulties are insurmountable; and so on. What we cannot understand is why someone should feel that way with little or no reason.

Labile Emotions. Another psychotic symptom is the expression of labile emotions. The patient may shift suddenly from a state of good humor to one of sudden anger, followed shortly, perhaps, by a state of depression. For example, "The patient will switch in one second from exaggerated, intense, angry agitation with cursing, screaming, jumping about, to an exaggeratedly erotic, happy mood, only to become tearful and sad a few minutes later" (EB, p. 43). The sudden unpredictable shift between radically different emotions, especially in the absence of corresponding changes in external circumstances or events, violates the emotional logic that underlies people's thoughts on the subject.

Purpose

Human actions, we ordinarily assume, are not random events; rather, they are guided by a sense of purpose. When people speak or act, they do so in order to achieve some end, aim, or goal. When people say that they cannot understand why a man acted as he did, they often mean that they did not understand the purpose of the behavior. It is for this reason that purposeless behavior is so often viewed as psychotic.

Bleuler provides a number of examples of purposeless behavior among schizophrenics:

> More advanced cases show the habit of collecting all sorts of objects, useful as well as useless, with which they fill their apartments so that there was hardly any room to move around. Ultimately this collecting mania becomes so utterly senseless that their pockets are always crammed full of pebbles, pieces of wood . . . rags and all kinds of other trash. (EB, p. 93)

Many of the symptoms of catatonia appear to be completely purposeless. For example, a patient goes around with a silly grin on his face all the time. Another walks around in a Napoleonic pose. A third spends years rubbing his right hand over his left thumb.

Sometimes we can understand what the person is trying to do but cannot for the life of us imagine why anyone would want to do it. "Factitious disorders" (DSM, pp. 315–20) are an example. The person with a factitious disorder devotes all his efforts to attempting to get *into* the hospital and staying there. He may complain of pain, such as stomach aches, which probably do not exist; may intentionally produce abscesses on the skin; or may avoid telling a doctor that he is allergic to a drug in order to create the noxious physical reaction. Although the means used to gain his ends are fairly reasonable, what defies comprehension is why any physically healthy person should have such a powerful wish to get into, and continue to remain in, a hospital.

Free Will

Whatever the resolution of the free will and determinism controversy, people operate on the assumption that human actions are products of free will. Most behavior is assumed to be under voluntary control. At the same time, people recognize that some behavior does not appear to be a matter of volition. Even a nonsmoker can understand why a smoker, despite his sincere desire to do so, is unable to give up cigarettes. Other acts also may not be freely chosen: people may lose their tempers, become overly excited, or experience fits of jealousy even though they do not want to.

Loss of volitional control, then, does not necessarily puzzle observers. What baffles them are the *types* of impulses or desires that cannot be controlled.

The *compulsions* are illustrative. Compulsives feel that they *must* act in certain ways, even though the behavior is contrary to their wills. An example is that of a girl who felt compelled to turn off the light six times every night and who had to make sure that her shoes were lined up in a certain way before she could fall asleep at night (CB, p. 480). Another is that of a woman who felt compelled to arrange her clothes and shoes in the closet until they were "perfect" and could not leave her room until things were absolutely right (CB, p. 170). A third example is that of a student who always sat in the third seat of the fifth row in each classroom, went out of his way to avoid certain buildings on campus, and felt compelled to line up his books and pencils in a certain way before he would begin studying (CB, p. 70). Most people find such compulsions impossible to understand.

Still more puzzling are instances in which individuals feel that external forces direct their actions without the mediation of their own thoughts. In these cases, the sense of volition vanishes entirely. The phenomenon of "delusions of control" is illustrative. The delusion of being controlled involves "the belief or experience that his feelings, impulses, thoughts, or actions are not his own and are imposed on him by some external force." For example, "A man claimed that his words were not his own but those of his father. A student believed that his actions were under the control of a yogi" (DSM, p. 395).

Self and Identity

The sense of self is an omnipresent and universal feature of human experience. The self, whether in the forefront or background of attention, is with us whatever we do, accompanies us wherever we go. Hence, the idea of a person without a sense of self is almost impossible to grasp.

Yet several mental disorders involve precisely such a loss of self or identity. One of these is called *depersonalization*. Campbell (1981, p. 163) defines depersonalization as "a nonspecific syndrome in which the patient feels he has lost his personal identity, that he is different and strange and unreal." Depersonalized people may experience themselves as separated, detached, or disconnected from themselves, as onlookers of their own actions. They may not know who they are; feel that what they are doing is being done by someone else; or feel "outside" themselves. They may also feel that some part of the body is not real ("Cotard's syndrome"). Even the most fundamental identity—sex identity—may be lost.

Frequently accompanying the experience of depersonalization is the feeling of derealization. This is the feeling that what is happening is not actually taking place—that things are happening as though in a dream.

Certain other dissociative disorders also involve the loss of, or confusion about, the sense of self. In the case of Multiple Personality Disorder, the individual has two or more personalities which tend to alternate with one another. The two personalities are likely to have different names and often different traits. "For example, a quiet, retiring spinster may alternate with a flamboyant, promiscuous bar habitue; or a person may have one personality that responds to aggression with childlike fright and flight, another that responds with masochistic submission, and yet another that responds with counterattack" (DSM, p. 270). Sometimes personalities are aware of one another, sometimes not. So completely ingrained is the assumption of the unity of personality (the single self) that observers are at a total loss to understand such a phenomenon.

Psychogenic fugue also exemplifies the loss of identity. A person suddenly travels to a different community and assumes a new identity without being aware of his previous identity. For example, a man who had been a middle-level manager at a large manufacturer disappeared one day and appeared in another town 200 miles away. When found in the new locality, he had a different name and was working as short-order cook in a diner. Although he knew what town he was in and what the current date was, he could recall nothing of his past life. When his wife met him, he did not recognize her (CB, pp. 215–16).

The identity disorder that is probably the most difficult to understand is the belief system known as "nihilistic delusion." In these cases, the individual believes that the self or part of the self does not exist. The patient may be convinced that he has no brain, lacks internal organs, and so on, or may even believe that he is dead.

Such TEBs are judged to be psychotic. To be unaware of who or what one is, to have the sense that one is outside oneself—such experiences are beyond us.

Erotic Arousal

Erotic attraction to an adult member of the other sex appears so biologically and socially natural that people are usually unable to understand why or how certain other stimuli can be sexually arousing.

Some people, for example, are only able to gain sexual arousal by exposing their genitals to strangers (exhibitionism). In other cases, men can only become sexually aroused by certain inanimate objects, such as bras, underpants, shoes, boots, or other apparel (fetishism). In still other instances, only prepubescent children are able to arouse sexual excitement in the individual (pedophilia). In some instances, people are able to experience sexual excitement only under certain conditions, such as "sexual masochism" ("being humiliated, beaten, bound, or otherwise made to suffer") or "sexual sadism" (torturing or humiliating the sexual object) (DSM, pp. 286–87). Still others can only experience arousal through cross-dressing (transvestism). In addition, some people can be aroused by other objects, such as corpses or animals, or by engaging in telephone scatologia (making lewd telephone calls).

On the basis of their own experiences, the experiences of people they know, or their general knowledge of human behavior, most people find such behavior to be incomprehensible. They cannot imagine how anyone can find a corpse, an animal, a boot, or a prepubescent child sexually arousing, or how torturing and humiliating someone or subjecting oneself to such torture and humiliation can possibly produce such an effect. It is essentially because of its incomprehensibility, not its deviance, that such behavior is considered mentally ill.

Interpersonal Estrangement

One of the main reasons why schizophrenia is considered to be such a serious disorder is that it is frequently characterized by social withdrawal. Schizophrenics often seem to retreat into their own thoughts, to lose interest in other people, to develop a radical detachment from the world. It is no accident that such people are often described as "loners"; their relationships with people are often formal and distant. They seem to live in a world apart from others. Human beings are so deeply involved with other people in virtually every conceivable way that it is almost impossible to conceive of people who are almost completely detached from other human beings.

Equally difficult to understand is the social insensitivity that sometimes characterizes the mentally ill. The individual seems to have lost the ability to take the role of the other. Such role-taking deficiency is evident in people's indifference to, a lack of awareness of, other people's anticipated or actual responses to their behavior. Some schizophrenics may talk to strangers at great length without being aware that the stranger considers this behavior to be an intrusion, has no interest in what the speaker is saying, has other things on his mind, and so on.

Manics often exhibit similar behavior. A manic may overhear people discussing some topic and may immediately enter the conversation, telling the bewildered listeners with absolute assurance what the real facts are and where the truth lies. A manic may also "give advice on matters about which he or she has no special knowledge, such as how to run a mental hospital or the United Nations" (DSM, p. 215). At times they will be found passing out candy, money, or advice to people in the street. It is not unusual for manics to phone or visit people in the middle of the night in order to tell them about certain exciting or ambitious plans they are concocting.

Bleuler's work is rife with examples of schizophrenics' obliviousness to others' mental events. For example, a teacher writes a letter to the school authorities asking that he be reinstated in his job, but much of the letter is devoted to insulting the people to whom his plea is directed. A woman patient begins to sing at a hospital concert; unfortunately, once she gets started, she will not stop. Despite hisses and catcalls from the audience, she continues on to the end of her performance and seems quite pleased by the entire experience. People find such behavior baffling. They are unable to take the role of those who are unable to take the role of others.

The Critical Feature

It is thus apparent that the manifestations of mental disorder are many and varied. These examples are not exhaustive; there are many other kinds that I have not mentioned. Varied though they are in form and content, I believe that they have but one characteristic in common. This is the fact that observers cannot understand them, cannot comprehend the internal mental events that are their source.

It is role-taking failure, not some other feature of the thought, emotion, or behavior, that leads to the judgment of mental illness. This is shown by the fact that *as soon as the TEB becomes comprehensible, it immediately becomes sane.* In other words, whether a TEB is sane or insane is not dependent on the nature of the TEB but on the observer's ability to grasp the mental events underpinning it. Let me attempt to illustrate this point by considering behavior, thought, and feeling separately.

Behavior. Take the case of a man who intentionally burns down a building. Is this act sane or insane? It depends on whether we are able to understand the actor's motives. If he does it in order to collect the insurance or to exact vengeance on someone who has done him harm, then we judge it to be sane. But if he does it because he is overtaken by an irresistible impulse to set the fire, then we diagnose him as a pyromaniac. What make the same behavior both sane or insane is the ability or inability to understand the reason for the actor's behavior. The fact that an insane act can instantly become a sane one the moment we understand the mental events underlying it clearly demonstrates that the insanity is a function of role-taking success or failure.

Thought. Like disordered behavior, disordered thought is also based on role-taking failure. Indeed, in the psychiatric view, it is the disordered mind that underlies the disordered behavior that is the root of the problem. Yet, as with behavior, the same thought can be both sane and insane. People divorced from reality may be considered sane and those in contact with it insane. Prior to the fifteenth century, the view that the earth was round would have called into question a person's sanity. In medieval Europe, the belief in witches was sane, whereas today the same beliefs may be considered insane. When Galileo contended that objects of different weight fell at the same rate of speed, it was not he but his contemporaries who were out of contact with reality. Whether a thought is sane or insane, then, is not a reflection of its correspondence with reality but of its comprehensibility to most members of society.

Emotion. As with behavior and thought, the identical emotion can be instantly transmuted from insanity to sanity as soon as the actor's mental events are understood. Is intense fear or profound depression sane or insane? That depends on whether we understand the reasons for it. Consider the feeling of fear or anxiety. If a person experiences intense fear at riding in an elevator or walking in a crowd, we would consider this to be a sign of mental disorder. But if the same emotion is experienced when someone threateningly points a loaded gun at this person, no one would judge this to be a symptom of mental disorder. If I feel calm and contented when lying peacefully on a sunny beach, this emotion is perfectly normal. But if I am equally calm and contented when a fire is raging all around me, then the emotion would be considered symptomatic of mental disorder. (Bleuler reports instances of seriously disordered schizophrenics behaving this way.) A patient with a serious illness may experience the most intense anxiety without being considered mentally disturbed. The death of a spouse, the loss of a livelihood, the failure of one's plans may arouse deep feelings of depression without calling into question one's sanity. Insane emotions suddenly become sane ones, not because the emotion in itself has changed in any way but because the observer suddenly gains new insight into the actor's inner world.

Whether we are able to take the role of the other often depends on whether the actor can offer a convincing *reason* for the TEB. If a person explains that his reason for washing his hands twenty times a day is to protect himself against germs, we find it difficult to put ourselves in his shoes. But if we find out that he is a surgeon, then the incomprehensible behavior suddenly becomes comprehensible. When a person muttering non-sense syllables explains to us that he is a subject in a psychological experiment, the senseless behavior becomes sane. When I get down on all fours and begin barking like a dog, my students are baffled. But when I explain that the reason I am doing so is to demonstrate ethnomethodological principles, comprehension replaces mystification.

Delusions of reference and persecution are mentally disordered because patients are unable to supply plausible reasons for their persecutors' actions. They may offer such explanations as, "There are people who are jealous of him, who fear his commercial or sexual competition, or who out of meanness, out of pleasure in torturing, out of inquisitiveness or for some other private purposes, use him for experiments" (EB, p. 118).

It is thus apparent that the mental status of a TEB depends entirely on its comprehensibility. No TEB is in itself sane or insane; the sanity or insanity is a function of role-taking failure or success.

4

Comparison of Approaches

In this chapter I compare role-taking theory with the other views of mental disorder presented in Chapter 1. The purpose of this comparison is twofold. First, I will explain why many of these other conceptions enjoy such popularity among both popular and professional writers, and why they are thought to be the defining feature of mental disorder. A major reason, I shall suggest, is to be found in role-taking theory.

The second aim of this chapter is to highlight the difference between role-taking theory and two major societal reaction theories of mental disorder, namely, labeling theory and emotional deviance theory. A comparison of the role-taking and medical approaches will be reserved for the final chapter.

Alternative Conceptions

In Chapter 1 I noted that the following characteristics are often associated in people's minds with the idea of mental disorder: unpredictability, dangerousness, statistical abnormality, normative abnormality, strangeness, psychological distress, irrationality, and disability. I suggest, however, that it is not unpredictability, dangerousness, irrationality, and so on that makes TEBs mentally disordered; it is the breakdown in interpersonal understanding.

Unpredictability

Studies of public attitudes toward mental illness, I noted earlier, show that people tend to think of the mentally disordered as unpredictable. This is understandable, since schizophrenic patients often do display unpredictable behavior. But it is their incomprehensibility, not their unpredictability, that arouses in others' minds the suspicion of mental disorder. For example, if a student suddenly stands up in class and begins shouting at the top of his lungs, this behavior is certainly unexpected. But what calls into question the sanity of the act is not that it is unexpected but that it appears to be purposeless. Were we able to discern its purpose (say, the building is on fire), then we would consider the behavior to be eminently sane. Or assume that during a quiet conversation our companion suddenly yelps and begins to slap his body furiously and hop around "like a madman"—certainly unexpected behavior. But the behavior becomes comprehensible, and therefore sane, when we learn that a bee has just flown down his back and is trapped inside his clothing.

Why, then, does the public tend to think of mentally ill persons as unpredictable? The reason is that if we cannot understand what others are thinking, it is difficult to predict their behavior. Research on public attitudes toward mental illness (Nunnally 1961, p. 46) supports this view. According to Nunnally, unpredictability is a cornerstone of the public conception of psychosis. But Nunnally shows that for most people, the underlying connotation of unpredictability is lack of *understandability*. In people's minds, the concept of unpredictability connotes something mysterious, complicated, and strange (Nunnally 1961, p. 46). If other people's mental events baffle us, we are apt to think of them as unpredictable.

Dangerousness

That mentally disordered people are sometimes dangerous is undeniable. For example, in 1989 a young man entered an engineering college in Montreal and, railing wildly against feminism, proceeded to assassinate a number of young women before he finally committed suicide. Several years earlier, John Hinckley attempted to shoot President Reagan, wounding several people in the attempt.

Such events command an immense amount of attention in the mass media and doubtlessly contribute to the popular stereotype of the insane as dangerous. It is apparent, however, that what makes such behavior insane is not the fact that it is dangerous but that it is incomprehensible. In the Montreal case, the behavior appears to be utterly purposeless. That a young man might develop antifeminist views is understandable, but that he should resort to such an extreme method of expressing his opposition is incomprehensible. Hinckley attempted to shoot President Reagan because he was obsessed with the actress Jody Foster—certainly an unusual way to impress a woman.

The fact that behavior endangers others, then, is no indication that it is "insane." This is shown by the fact that as soon as a dangerous act becomes comprehensible, it is transmuted from the realm of insanity into sanity. If Hinckley's assassination attempt had been based on political ideology, he would not have been considered mentally ill. The perpetrators of the St. Valentine's Day massacre, in which members of one gang systematically exterminated the members of a rival gang, are judged to be sane.

One reason the mentally disordered are thought to be dangerous may be their assumed unpredictability. Unpredictable people make us uneasy;

they often arouse in us the feeling that we are in the presence of danger. If we have no idea what is going on in people's minds, we tend to become keyed up, alert, vigilant. I believe that Nunnally (1961, p. 46) is correct when he observes that "unpredictable behavior is frightening." We can thus understand why people tend to be somewhat afraid of psychotics.

Statistical Abnormality

A statistically abnormal TEB is one that is rare and unusual. That it should be seen as characteristic of mental illness is not surprising. Mentally disordered people often do exhibit highly unusual thoughts, feelings, and behaviors. One patient may stop speaking in the middle of a sentence; when he continues, it is to discuss an entirely different topic. Another patient may think that everyone on the street is talking about her.

Such behavior is certainly statistically abnormal. But that is not what makes it mentally disordered; it is its incomprehensibility. For example, imagine entering a room full of people and finding a woman screwing up her face, moving her arms and hands in strange ways, and remaining completely mute in the process. Certainly this is unusual behavior, and, in the absence of further information, we might call into question her mental status. But once we learn that she is playing charades, her behavior becomes sane.

The fact that a TEB is rare or unusual, then, is not in itself a sign of mental disorder. It is only disordered if people are unable to take the role of the actor. Other things equal, however, rare or unusual behavior is more likely to be experienced as hard to understand than common or familiar behavior. We can thus see why statistical abnormality should be associated in people's minds with mental illness.

Normative Abnormality

Normative abnormality refers to behavior that violates the rules or accepted practices of a society. Such behavior is judged to be wrong, inappropriate, or deviant. For example: "A well-educated young woman, whose illness is hardly noticeable suddenly moves her bowels before a whole social gathering and cannot comprehend the embarrassment which she causes among her friends" (EB, p. 64).

Although such behavior grossly violates the behavioral norms of society, it is not the normative abnormality or social inappropriateness that makes it psychotic; it is the patient's total obliviousness to other people's reactions. People are baffled by those who are unable to take the role of others.

Once again, incomprehensibility, rather than something else (in this case, inappropriateness), marks a behavior as deranged. As soon as the

TEB becomes comprehensible, the insanity is instantly converted into sanity. For example, failure to respond when addressed is socially inappropriate behavior and may call into question the individual's mental status. But when one discovers that the person is deaf, then the behavior, although it violates a social norm, is viewed as normal. These observations, however, also help us to understand why normative abnormality is often mistakenly equated with mental illness. In general, people experience little difficulty in understanding normative conformity, that is, they are rarely puzzled by socially appropriate behavior. It is when people violate the norms that an explanation is needed. It is for this reason that the suspicion of mental disorder is more likely to fall on deviant than on socially appropriate behavior.

Strangeness or Oddity

It is easy to understand why the examples of schizophrenic behavior presented in this book often strike people as "strange," "odd," "peculiar," or even "bizarre." What makes a TEB strange or peculiar, however, is not the TEB itself but our inability to understand the mental events underlying it. It is peculiar of me to twist my torso into a contorted position, but not if I am exercising. An odd grimace is no longer odd when we learn that the person has just eaten a piece of lemon.

Role-taking theory helps us understand why strange behavior is particularly likely to be considered psychotic. When we call an act peculiar, we assume that we are describing the act; but what we are actually describing is our own reaction to it. To say that someone's behavior is peculiar is to say that we are unable to grasp the other's point of view. The reason we are more likely to think of peculiar behavior as mentally disordered, then, is that peculiar behavior is behavior that we cannot completely understand.

Psychological Distress

It is undeniable that mentally disordered people often experience psychological distress. For example, consider the experience of someone undergoing a panic disorder. As described in DSM–III–R (p. 236):

> Panic attacks typically begin with the sudden onset of intense apprehension, fear, or terror. Often there is a feeling of impending doom. . . . The symptoms experienced during an attack are: shortness of breath (dyspnea) or smothering sensations; dizziness, unsteady feelings, or faintness; choking; palpitations or accelerated heart rate; trembling or shaking; sweating; nausea or abdominal distress; depersonalization or derealization; numbness or tingling sensations (paresthesias); . . . fear of dying; and fear of going crazy or doing something uncontrolled during the attack.

And yet it is not these painful feelings, that constitute the defining feature of the mental disorder. One can undergo equally distressing experiences without doubt being cast on one's mental status. The identical symptoms would be perfectly sane for a soldier undergoing bombardment for the first time; or for someone anticipating a life-threatening operation. What is not understandable is why someone should have such feelings when riding in an elevator, driving in the center lane on a highway, or walking on a crowded street. It is thus not the intensity of the psychological distress but the inexplicability of the reaction in light of the objective stimulus event that is the essence of the pathology.

The *absence* of psychological distress may also reflect disorder. The person who is unmoved by the loss of a spouse, parent, or friend, or who is unconcerned about his or her own illness or the illness of a loved one, may elicit doubts about his or her sanity.

Role-taking theory, however, helps us to understand why psychological distress is so often associated in people's minds with mental disorder. The reason is that when people are unable to take the role of the other, their connection to other human beings is severed. It is hard to contemplate anything more terrifying or painful than the condition of being completely cut off from other human beings. Role-taking theory thus helps us to understand why people are likely to think that the mentally disordered must suffer terribly, and, in turn, to believe that this suffering is the defining feature of the disorder. Indeed, the break with society that represents a core feature of psychotic TEBs is in fact a major cause of suffering for the mentally ill. It is thus easy to see why people should erroneously think of such suffering as the defining feature of mental disorder.

Irrationality

Many, if not most, symptoms of mental disorder strike us as irrational. Consider the behavior of one of Bleuler's patients:

> A patient, who had become deaf but who could speak very well, always wrote down everything she wished to say, but she insisted that we give her only oral answers, thereby making conversation completely impossible. She would also hide her own and other patients' handkerchiefs whenever she could, and then complain and protest that the nurse had stolen them. (EB, p. 194)

To most people, the meaning of irrationality seems self-evident. According to Fingarette (1972, pp. 183–84):

> . . . we would say it is irrational . . . to giggle or chuckle pleasedly at the sight of a mangled human body, to feel pleasure at the death of a loved one, to feel gloomy upon succeeding in an important venture, to step nonchalantly and knowingly in front of a racing train, to desire to maim oneself.

But what makes these TEBs irrational? No criteria are presented. It seems to me that the common element is the observer's inability to make sense of the actor's point of view.

To say that an act is irrational means that we cannot comprehend the reason for it. However, if we can find a reason for it, then the act, although it remains the same, becomes rational. For example, a normally prudent man suddenly goes on a spending binge, throwing his money around wantonly and presenting outrageously expensive gifts to people he hardly knows. We call such behavior (which is symptomatic of a manic episode) irrational. But when we discover that he has just been told that he has three months to live, the behavior suddenly becomes rational. The reason for his behavior is clear: he can't take it with him. Irrationality, then, does not inhere in the thought, emotion, or behavior itself; it is, rather, a reflection of the observer's inability to find the reason for it.

Role-taking theory thus helps us to understand why people so often equate mental illness with irrationality. To call behavior irrational is equivalent to saying that we are unable to understand the reason for it. Irrationality, like mental illness, stems from role-taking failure.

Disability

DSM-III-R uses the term *disability* to refer primarily to interference with social functioning. People afflicted with mental disorders are usually unable to carry on their normal family, occupational, or other social roles. Since disability does tend to be characteristic of the mentally disordered, we can understand why it is often judged to be its defining feature.

But the question is; *Why* is disability so likely to be characteristic of mental disorder? The answer is, I suggest, that role-taking failure erects an insuperable barrier between human beings. If people cannot understand what others are thinking or why they are speaking or acting as they do, it becomes impossible for them to align their actions with those of others (Blumer 1969). Human interaction is aborted; it comes to a dead halt.

That a person who experiences a communication breakdown should experience difficulty in functioning effectively in important institutional areas is inevitable. Consider, for example, the matter of *family* functioning. Relatives often report how difficult it is to live with the mentally ill. Psychotics are often highly autistic; they live in a separate world of thoughts and feelings. As a result of their interpersonal estrangement, the reciprocal understanding that is so essential for successful human interaction is lost. Divorce, separation, marital conflict, or failure to fulfill one's family roles are almost inevitable accompaniments of role-taking failure.

It is also virtually inevitable that the mentally disordered will experience *occupational* difficulties. Although there probably is a place for occupational isolates in our society (night watchmen, for example), in most cases the organization of business and industry is such that people must work with others. In order for people's occupational efforts to mesh, they must be able to interact successfully. The absence of "mutual perspectivism" (Selman 1980)—the reciprocal role-taking process—rules out the possibility of such successful interaction.

In sum, if one cannot understand another's viewpoint, one is at a loss as to how to deal with that person. Husbands and wives, parents and children, supervisors and employees, patients and doctors, lawyers and clients—all must be able to take account of one another's viewpoints if their interactions are to be productive and successful. That the inability to take the role of the other should produce difficulties in marriage, work, relations with children, neighbors, relatives, and so on is, I suggest, best explained by role-taking theory.

Nonverbal Communication

Miller and Jaques (1988), it will be recalled, suggested that the defining feature of mental disorder is the presence of certain patterns of nonverbal communication which disrupt social encounters. The main types they focus on are those behaviors involving the violation of spatiotemporal rules. Since they are found among schizophrenics, we can see why some writers should fasten on such behavior as the defining feature. Some patients may speak too rapidly, others too slowly; some may come too close, others may stand too far away. While carrying on a conversation, a patient may gaze off into the distance. Schizophrenics may also violate the turn-taking rules of conversation. Such behavior, it is apparent, is likely to damage the social encounter.

What Miller and Jaques fail to ask, however, is *why* these violations of spatiotemporal rules are considered to be signs of mental illness. The reason, I suggest, is that observers are unable to understand the mental processes underlying the behavior. Yet once they do, these violations of spatiotemporal rules are no longer viewed as symptomatic of mental illness. They become sane when, for example, we discover that the reason a man stands so close is that he does not want others nearby to overhear what he is saying; or that he considers such closeness to be appropriate for the soft murmurings of love.

It is thus evident that there are many perfectly sane reasons for violating spatiotemporal rules. A person may speak very loudly because the listener is hard of hearing. A professor may speak very rapidly because she is eager to finish an important point before the end of the class. A man may speak abnormally slowly because the listener has a poor command of the language. Clearly, it is not the violation of spatiotemporal rules, but the observer's inability to understand this behavior, that is the basis for designating it as mentally disordered.

Miller and Jaques have also failed to address the reason why the violation of spatiotemporal rules so seriously disrupts the social encounter. According to role-taking theory, it is because, in the absence of further explanation or clarification, such violations are incomprehensible to others. If we are unable to understand why the other person is standing so close, or talking so loud or gazing off into the distance, then we are mystified about the content of their thoughts. Inevitably such behavior disrupts or even aborts the conversation. Miller and Jaques are thus correct in contending that the violation of rules of time and space may be destructive of communication, but they overlook the fact that the reason for this destruction is people's inability to grasp the mental events underlying these violations.

In sum, mental disorder has been subject to a remarkably wide range of theories. Most of these theories capture some characteristic feature of the phenomenon. Thus, it is probably true that the mentally disordered are more likely than normal people to exhibit thoughts, emotions, and behaviors that are statistically abnormal, socially inappropriate, strange or bizarre, irrational, psychologically distressing, socially disabling, and so on. But it is not the statistical abnormality, social inappropriateness, strangeness, or irrationality that makes these TEBs mentally disordered. It is, rather, that statistically rare, socially inappropriate, and socially disabling TEBs are more likely to be incomprehensible to others. The underlying element in all of these symptoms is role-taking failure.

Societal Reaction Conceptions

Two of the most prominent societal reaction theories of mental disorder are labeling theory (Scheff 1966, 1974, 1984) and emotional deviance theory (Thoits 1985). These theories root mental illness in the social interaction process. Role-taking theory shares this orientation. There are, however, important differences among these approaches. The remainder of this chapter will be devoted to a discussion of these differences.

Labeling Theory

Labeling theory and role-taking theory differ from one another on a number of dimensions, the most important being the conception of the defining feature of mental disorder. Labeling theory holds that the defining feature is residual rule-breaking, whereas role-taking views it as thought-reading failure.

Scheff's (1966, 1974, 1984) argument, it will be recalled, is that there are many forms of deviance in society. Some of these are classified as crime, some as perversion, some as prostitution, some as drunkenness, some as immorality, some simply as bad manners. Those that do not fall into any of these categories (residual deviance) are called mental illness.

According to labeling theory, then, the distinction between mental illness and other types of deviance is based on a culturally arbitrary system of classification. Robbery is called crime and the flight of ideas is called schizophrenia for the same reason that one man is called Henry and the other, John. Similarly, lying, deception, and exploitation are called immorality, whereas thought insertion and auditory hallucinations are called schizophrenia because that is how these types of behavior happen to be classified in our society.

Role-taking theory, by contrast, holds that these distinctions are by no means culturally arbitrary. Rather, they rest on a clearly specified principle: the ability to enter the mind of the other and to make successful attributions. The reason we call some kinds of behavior crime and other kinds insanity is that we feel we can make successful attributions in the first case but not in the second. Each of us understands what it is to want something that is not ours; we have succeeded in restraining ourselves from taking it because of conscience or fear. We therefore have no difficulty in understanding crime, in putting ourselves in the role of the criminal, in understanding his underlying motives. As Gibbs (1990, p. 974) expresses it, "No American is truly baffled by robbery."

One might think that the difference between crime and insanity is the fact that a law has been violated, but that is not the case: insane acts may also violate the law. Nor does the difference lie in the damage inflicted on the victim, since sane and legal acts (e.g., war, police actions) often cause more damage than insane ones. It is simply that we define the act as criminal when we feel we understand the person's motives or vantage point.

Nor is the distinction between immorality and insanity a matter of arbitrary social classification. Nothing is more comprehensible than immorality. None of us is likely to have any trouble understanding why someone may wish to lie, cheat, or exploit. Such behavior may be deplorable, but there is no question that it is sane. Few people consider marital infidelity, embezzlement, or bribery to be insane; it may be immoral, but it is all too easy to understand. Only when we are unable to understand the immoral behavior from the actor's point of view do we question the person's mental status. It is easy to understand, for example, why someone lies for advantage; we call such behavior immorality. But it is difficult to understand why someone lies for no purpose; we call such behavior pathological lying.

In sum, whereas the labeling position views mental illness as the violation of an unclassifiable mélange of "left-over rules," role-taking theory argues that there is a definite principle underlying the distinction between mental illness and other types of deviance and specifies what that principle is, namely, the breakdown in interpersonal understanding.

Role-taking theory also calls into question labeling's conception of social deviance. From the examples presented by Scheff, it is clear that deviance, including mental disorder, is viewed in a normative sense. A deviant is someone who has offended the mores and whose behavior is classified as "bad." For example, the societal reaction to crime, infidelity, lying, perversion, bad manners, drunkenness, and so on is to deplore such behavior—to consider it to be wrong, evil, or undesirable. The characteristic societal response to such behavior, as Durkheim (1964) has stressed, is punishment, expressed in rejection, ostracism, condemnation, ridicule, disapproval, and so on.

But if mental illness, like these other types of norm violation, were simply viewed as wrong, bad, or evil, then one would expect the reaction of society to it to be outrage and condemnation. If, on the other hand, mental disorder is actually role-taking failure, then the reaction to it should be puzzlement and confusion. I believe that the latter response is the characteristic one. For example, if a person's speech is characterized by non sequiturs, flight of ideas, or irrelevant associations, the typical reaction is to view it not as bad, evil, or reprehensible, but as baffling or incomprehensible. For most people there is a recognizable difference between behavior that is baffling but not evil and behavior that is evil but not baffling.

Furthermore, if mental disorder, like other forms of deviance, were simply bad, then one would expect society to punish the violator—to fine, jail, ostracize, or otherwise inflict harm on him or her (Becker 1963). If, on the other hand, mental disorder is incomprehensible, then the inclination is to attempt to effect such change in the individual as to make him or her comprehensible to others. This, I believe, is what society tends to do. It is no accident, after all, that society establishes different institutions for the criminal and the mentally disordered. For the criminal it provides prisons, equipped with barred cells, surrounded by walls, and staffed with armed guards. For the insane, society provides mental hospitals, community mental health centers, wards of general hospitals, and so on, staffing these organizations with doctors, nurses, aides, and related personnel. Clearly, societal reactions to mental illness and to other kinds of "rule-breaking" are different. The reason is that it is not norm violation but role-taking failure that is the foundation of mental disorder.

Indeed, it is questionable whether mental illness should be considered deviance at all. It might be more appropriate to view it as *deviation*—a social handicap with which certain people are burdened. In this respect, it might join other types of handicaps such as low intelligence, physical weakness, diminutive stature, homeliness, clubbed foot, and so on. These may be considered undesirable but there is no inclination to inflict punishment or to hold people responsible for them.

Finally, the role-taking and labeling approaches hold different views about the maladaptive nature of mental disorder. The labeling view is that once society, through some official certifying agency or agent, formally identifies someone as mentally ill, society responds to the individual in these negative terms. In time, the individual internalizes the label and comes to adopt a corresponding view of the self.

The wide-ranging consequences of labeling have been described by many labeling theorists (Schur 1971; Lemert 1972; Scheff 1966, 1974, 1975, 1984). Although not denying these consequences, role-taking theory identifies an additional, even more consequential, source of maladjustment that labeling overlooks. These are the consequences of role-taking failure. Human communication and cooperation depend on taking the role of the other, on seeing matters from the other's point of view. If other people cannot comprehend what is going on in the actor's mind, they cannot communicate with him or her.

The inability of others to take the role of the actor is totally destructive of meaningful human communication, which depends on our anticipation of other people's responses to our words or actions. If we have no comprehension of what is going on in the other's mind—why he stares into space, what his disconnected words mean, why he flies into a rage without provocation—then the human bond is snapped. Social maladjustment—the inability to function successfully in society—is inevitable. That loss of job, marital rupture, or destruction of friendships should be the experience of the mentally disordered is readily understood. Role-taking theory helps us to understand why mental illness inevitably produces profound social maladjustment.

Emotional Deviance

Thoits's (1985) theory, it will be recalled, is that people are identified, and identify themselves, as mentally disordered when they violate the emotional norms of society. Thoits points out that an elaborate system of emotional rules is to be found in society. Different emotions are expected (indeed, demanded) of people in different situations and of incumbents of different social positions. Thoits thus suggests that the failure to exhibit the socially appropriate emotions may call into question the actor's mental status.

Thoits has provided some insightful observations of some of the social and cultural conditions that may produce emotional deviance:

1. Many emotional reactions are spontaneous and involuntary (e.g., the shocked feeling at seeing a grossly deformed person). Even though considered wrong, there is nothing one can do about them.

2. Certain situations arouse conflicting emotions in people. A person may experience sorrow at the death of a loved one and simultaneous relief that the person's suffering is at an end. Yet to be pleased rather than saddened is to violate an emotional norm.

3. The foundation of an emotion is a state of physiological arousal.

This arousal is the product of hormonal infusions in the bloodstream. These physiological phenomena may persist long after the stimulus that triggered them is past. For example, if someone is frightened, the feeling may persist long after the immediate cause is gone. Similarly, although it is socially appropriate to manifest and experience pleasure when guests arrive, it may be difficult to do so in the midst of a battle royal with one's spouse. Yet to greet arriving guests with a fierce scowl is to violate an emotional norm.

4. Stress situations can produce inappropriate feelings. Thoits has discussed some of the structurally based sources of stress: role conflict, role strain, role overload, status inconsistency, role transitions (especially unscheduled or unexpected transitions), and so on. Because of such stresses, for example, a mother may fail to experience the feeling of love toward her children that society demands of an incumbent of her status.

These observations are enlightening. But role-taking theory, I suggest, shows why the chief strength of Thoits's argument is at the same time its chief weakness. This is the fact that whenever people *recognize* that particular instances of emotional deviance are attributable to involuntary reactions, conflicting emotions, persistence of hormonal infusions, or any of the many causes of social stress, they do *not* judge the reaction to be mentally disordered. In other words, it is precisely for the reasons set forth by Thoits that people do *not* consider such emotional deviance to be mental illness. Implicitly or explicitly, people are aware of the operation of the social influences described by Thoits. When the host continues to seethe with anger after the guests arrive; when the medical student responds with revulsion at handling bodily wastes (Smith and Kleinman 1989); when the individual feels shock at encountering the deformed person (Goffman 1963)—these responses may violate emotional rules but they are not considered to be mentally disordered, either by the individual or by society generally. Although people may deplore such violations of emotional rules, these violations, being understandable, are considered eminently sane. It is only the kinds of emotional deviance that defy the thought-reading abilities of outside observers that are likely to call into question the mental status of the individual.

Labeling, emotional deviance, and role-taking are all societal reaction theories of mental disorder. They all agree that the mystery of mental illness does not reside exclusively within the individual psyche, but is to be found in society's reaction to certain kinds of behavior. But these three theories hold different views about the social influences that play a role in mental disorder. The tendency of some writers to speak of *the* sociological approach to mental disorder is thus inappropriate. There are several competing sociological approaches that can be counterposed to one another and that appear to be worthy of consideration.

5
Role-Taking, Reflexivity, and Self-Referral

R ole-taking, I have stressed, is a dyadic event, an event involving an observer and an actor. But if this is so, then role-taking theory encounters a major difficulty, namely, how is it possible for people to consider *themselves* to be mentally disordered? (Thoits 1985; Rotenberg 1974). Can the individual be both the observer and the person observed? Is it possible for a person to be unable to comprehend his or her own internal mental events and on that basis conclude that he or she is mentally disordered? If this were so, then one would have to contend that social interaction processes take place *within* the individual.

That is the argument that will be advanced in this chapter. Self-referral, I will suggest, is made possible by the paradoxical fact that the individual may at times be unable to take the role of the self. Although only one individual is involved, self-referral nevertheless remains an instance of the breakdown of interpersonal understanding.

Not all self-referral, of course, is based on the inability to comprehend one's own thoughts. People seek psychotherapy for many different reasons. Therapists in training (didactic analysis) want to improve their understanding of the analytic experience; others seek therapy because it is the fashionable thing to do. But most enter psychotherapy because they are unable to comprehend their own internal mental events.

The question is, How is it possible for people to be unable to take their own roles, to be unable to understand their own points of view? The answer, I will suggest, is to be found in the uniquely reflexive character of the human organism. In order to understand this point, it is first necessary to delve more deeply into the nature of human reflexivity and self-awareness.

Reflexivity: The Development of Self-Awareness

Reflexivity refers to the process of an entity acting back upon itself. Mead (1934) and Cooley (1902) clearly showed that reflexivity among human beings is rooted in the social process, particularly the process of taking the role of the other and seeing the self from the other's perspective. It is by

84

virtue of reflexivity that human beings develop an awareness of self. The self-aware person is both knower and object of knowledge (Rosenberg 1986b).

Whether the human being's awareness of the self is innate or solely a product of social experience is still a matter of dispute. Kagan (1981) contends that self-awareness in humans is a result of the unfolding of a given biological potential. Most symbolic interactionists (e.g., Reynolds 1990; Hewitt 1990), on the other hand, believe that self-awareness is a product of social interaction.

The evidence, in my opinion, supports the view that the development of a sense of self involves the joint operation of biological and social interactional influences. This evidence comes from research on primates and human infants. In a classic study, Gallup and Suarez (1986) placed young chimpanzees in cages containing full-length mirrors. Some of the chimpanzees remained in the cage alone whereas others shared the cage with other chimpanzees. Nine days later the animals were anaesthetized, and red dye markings were placed on an eyebrow and an ear of each one. The animals were returned to the mirrored cages, and investigators observed how often each chimpanzee pointed to, scratched, or showed other signs of awareness of the red markings.

Several important findings emerged. First, many of the animals showed evidence of self-recognition by scratching the dye on their own ear or eyebrow instead of scratching at the image in the mirror. This suggested that they were not simply responding to the image as an objective stimulus in the environment but were identifying the image that they saw in the mirror with a self. Second, this self-recognition appeared among chimpanzees that shared cages, not the chimps that occupied cages alone.

Social interaction, then, is essential to the development of self-awareness. At the same time, the evidence suggests that certain biological preconditions must be present. Gallup conducted this same investigation with a large number of other primates—rhesus monkeys, spider monkeys, macaques, baboons, gibbons—and found that self-recognition appeared in only two species: chimpanzees and orangutans.

Does this mean that chimpanzees are equipped with certain essential biological equipment that the other primates lack? There is evidence to suggest that they do. According to Hamburg, Coelho, and Adams (1974, p. 407):

Evidence from several lines of biological research indicates that the chimpanzee has a closer relationship to man than any other living animal. Important new discoveries have revealed close similarity between man and chimpanzee in chromosomes, blood proteins, immune responses and DNA. Moreover, continuing neuro-anatomical research has shown increasingly that the circuitry of man's brain resembles more closely that of the chimpanzee than it does that of any other species, including other apes and monkeys.

Obviously it is not possible to conduct such experimental studies with humans. Still, research with infants indicates that human self-awareness depends on both biological maturation and social interaction. The methodology of this research is similar to that used with the primates (Lewis and Brooks-Gunn 1979). Investigators had mothers, in the course of handling their babies, unobtrusively rub some rouge across the baby's face, producing a large red blotch on the infant's nose. The child is then placed in a playpen facing a large mirror. Infants, of course, have seen their images in the mirror many times. The question is, Do they know that this image refers to themselves, or do they simply respond to this image as the picture of a baby? Lewis and Brooks-Gunn reasoned that if the image were viewed as an object in the environment, then the infant would point to the nose in the mirror. But if they interpreted the image as referring to themselves, then they would point to their own noses.

Lewis and Brooks-Gunn found that the tendency to point to one's own nose was strongly correlated with age. Studying ninety-six children between nine and twenty-four months of age, they found that, before fifteen months, virtually none of the children showed any evidence of self-awareness; that is, none pointed to their own noses rather than to the noses in the mirror. The latter response, in fact, did not become the modal one until about twenty-one months of age (Lewis and Brooks-Gunn 1979, p. 43). Thus, even an extremely primitive self-concept appears to be absent in the early months of life.

The development of self-awareness, then, depends on the existence of a certain biological potential, stage of maturation, and ongoing social process of interaction. But it is of interest to note that it is at this age that the *semiotic* function—the ability to use signs and symbols—emerges in infancy. The development of self-awareness thus appears to coincide with the development of language. Although a complete understanding of the connection between the two is not available for this life stage, it is clear that, at later stages of development, language and communication play a critical role in the development of self-awareness.

Whenever an individual, in whole or in part, is the object of his or her cognition, he or she exemplifies the phenomenon of reflexivity. When the baby looking into the mirror points with surprise at its red nose, it reveals the ability to view the self as a distinct object. In contrast to most of nature, it has achieved the remarkable feat of being both subject and object; the viewer and the object viewed are the same person. Once this occurs, its fate is sealed. It has parted company with its animal forbears. Although other animals have consciousness, we stand virtually alone in nature in having *self*-consciousness. In the course of life, this development will be a source of both joy and sorrow to us, but there is no turning back. We have no option but to live with it.

That the child of eighteen to twenty-one months has developed some degree of self-awareness does not mean that he or she is now in possession of a full-fledged self-concept. A self-concept develops slowly. A lot of water will flow under the bridge before the complex and sophisticated self-concept structure and set of self-objectification processes that characterize more mature minds will come into being. But it is in the gross and primitive form of such self-recognition that the first glimmerings of these complex structures and processes are to be found.

From Social Exterior to Psychological Interior

What do children see when they look at themselves? Research on child development indicates that, in the early years, children's self-concepts consist largely of visible, exterior elements. Only later does the self gradually come to incorporate more and more invisible, interior elements. For example, when asked, "Who knows best what you really feel and think deep down inside? . . . What does this person know about you that others do not?" younger children tend to answer in terms of overt, visible, external, and public characteristics. The child's reply will usually focus on behavior; talents, abilities, or accomplishments; certain objective facts (e.g., physical characteristics or social identity elements); and similar kinds of visible information.

When we turn to adolescence, the picture changes radically. Although adolescent self-concepts also include overt and visible elements (adolescents, for example, are greatly concerned with physical appearance), they differ from children's in incorporating a much larger proportion of interior elements. In response to the question asking respondents what they are like "deep down inside," the majority of older children cite general thoughts and feelings, specific interpersonal feelings, or private wishes, desires, and aspirations (Rosenberg 1986b).

In sum, the data from a number of different studies (Rosenberg 1986b; Livesley and Bromley 1973; Secord and Peevers 1974; Montemayor and Eisen 1977; Shantz 1975; Damon and Hart 1988) are consistent: when asked to describe the self, the older child is decidedly more likely to answer in terms of a psychological interior—a world of emotions, attitudes, beliefs, wishes, motives—while the younger child is more likely to describe the self in terms of a social exterior—a world of action and activities (Keller, Ford, and Meacham 1978; Secord and Peevers 1974), objective facts, material possessions, and overt achievements.

It thus appears that developmental processes in person perception (described in Chapter 2) and developmental processes in self-perception follow a similar course. Just as young children are almost exclusively aware of the external features of other persons, so are they almost exclusively aware of external features of the self. And just as older children discover that other people possess a psychological interior, so they discover that they too possess a psychological interior.

Given these and other similarities, many writers (e.g., Livesley and Bromley 1973; Secord and Peevers 1974) have tended to treat person perception and self-perception as reflections of the same developmental processes. Indeed, some of the richest studies on self-perception are essentially person-perception studies, with self-perception included either as a buffer item or what appears to be little more than an afterthought.

Although the chronology and the development sequence in person perception and self-perception are much the same, I believe that there are fundamental differences between the two. The discovery of an internal world in other people—role-taking—is a prior stage and an essential precondition for the discovery of an internal world in the self.

The question is, How do people come to direct their attention to these internal events? How, in the words of William James (1950), does "thought become conscious of itself"?

Role-Taking and the Discovery of a Psychological Interior

In the child, the discovery of an internal world of thought and feeling emerges from role-taking and communication processes. At least two processes—reflected appraisals and social communication—operate to draw the child's internal events to his or her attention.

Reflected Appraisals

Role-taking represents the effort by the individual to see into the other's mind. But as one peers closely into the hidden worlds of other people, one gradually becomes aware that one of the objects that looms very large in the other's phenomenal field is oneself. Although this seems obvious, in fact this insight is not easily gained. In order to become fully social, according to Piaget (1928, p. 103): ". . . it is not enough for [the child] to enter into the point of view of others, he must also look at himself from the point of view of others, which is twice as difficult."

Whereas younger children are relatively oblivious to others' thoughts, preadolescence is a time of heightened and intensified role-taking. In preadolescence, Flavell (1968, p. 54) observes, "meticulous attention is given to the careful gauging of the thoughts and feelings of the other (especially toward oneself) . . ." It is this fact that gives adolescent social behavior its distinctive coloring. At this life stage, adolescents become almost obsessed with what others think of them. How do they look? Do others like them? What impression are they making? Many students of adolescence have remarked on the almost morbid and obsessive self-consciousness of young people.

The point is that the harder we strive to probe the other person's psychological interior, the more is our attention directed toward ourselves. The awareness of self thus emerges out of the process of taking the role of the other as our attention comes to focus on that object that looms so prominently in the other person's mind—ourselves.

But the strenuous effort to penetrate the internal worlds of others leads us to a still more profound level of self-discovery. For as we probe more deeply, we become more aware that the other person is doing the very same thing to us. We strive to discover their hidden thoughts, and learn that they are busily trying to discover ours. By looking carefully into their minds, our attention is drawn to our own internal world of thought and feeling. Awareness of our private invisible world thus comes to us from the outside in. The awareness that other people are seeking to probe one's own internal events emerges only at a relatively advanced developmental stage; according to Flavell, it rarely appears before middle childhood.

Flavell (1968, Chapter 2) has identified four stages in the development of role-taking. In one of his studies, children are asked to play a game in which the aim is to deceive the other person. The children are asked to describe the thought process of the opponent. At the earliest stage, the child can offer no explanation of what the other person is thinking or how that thought could affect his or her own behavior. At the second stage, the child shows awareness that the other person is attempting to solve the problem but not that the other person will attempt to fathom and take account of the child's own strategy. At the third stage, the child takes account of the other person's reasoning, considering the fact that this reasoning *will include consideration of the child's own thoughts.* At the fourth stage, the child becomes aware that the other will probe still more deeply into the child's own thoughts, seeking to divine his or her motives, strategies, and other internal mental processes.

Flavell found that most of the children in grades 2 through 5 remained at stage 2. They recognized that the other person had a viewpoint but failed to recognize that the viewpoint included a consideration of their own viewpoint. Stage 3 responses did not predominate until the seventh grade—preadolescence or early adolescence. The fourth stage appeared even later in adolescence.

The game of poker offers a good example of an advanced role-taking level. Suppose a man with a weak hand decides to raise heavily. Although this seems irrational, his purpose is to convince the other players that he has a strong hand. The reason he believes this strategy will be effective is that, taking the role of the other, he realizes that they are attempting to read his thoughts. Being unable to read his thoughts directly, they must depend on the inferences they draw from his overt behavior. They thus use the overt action of the raise to gain access to the covert cognition of the bettor. The bettor, taking the role of his opponents and making assumptions about how they will think, attempts to deceive them by betting heavily with a weak hand. It is possible, however, that the ploy will fail because the opponents decide that the bettor, taking account of their probable reasoning, is attempting to mislead them. Deciding that he is actually "bluffing," they match or exceed his bet. Each player, then, in taking the role of the other (reading the other's thoughts), is aware that the other is taking the role of the self (reading his or her own thoughts), and is making his betting decisions in accordance with these implicit assumptions.

One of the main influences drawing the child's attention to his or her own internal mental and emotional events, then, is the process of taking the role of the other. The more carefully the child probes and examines the other's mind, the more is the child's attention drawn to his or her own internal world. In this way, children come to achieve what Damon and Hart (1988) aptly describe as "an awareness of awareness." They become aware of their thoughts and feelings, so to speak, from the outside in. The social interaction process thus guides the mind toward the examination of its own contents.

There is a related social experience that also draws children's attention to their internal thoughts and feelings. This is the fact that other people, instead of struggling to penetrate the mystery of children's internal worlds, take the easy way out. They simply ask them directly. In the course of growing up, the child may be bombarded with such questions as "How do you feel?" "What do you think of the teacher?" "What do you want for Christmas?" "Do you like baseball?" "Are you worried about the history test?" "What is your favorite television program?" If children really listen and pay attention to such questions, they are driven irresistibly in the direction of reflexivity. Such questions ask them to conduct their own inspection of their internal world of thought and feeling and report back the results of their investigation. Children are forced to look inside, to explore the nooks and crannies of the mind. Attention is focused on one's own inner psychological events—beliefs, wants, preferences, fears, feelings, plans, intentions.

Once this occurs, the reflexive nature of the self—its essential duality—comes sharply to the fore. On the one side, the mind acting as the observer; on the other, the mind serving as the object of its own observation. The observing ego comes to adopt a detached stance toward its internal content—its beliefs, feelings, interests, attitudes, values, wishes, motives, physical sensations, or any other feature of the internal world.

Other people's questions are thus a major source of self-discovery. But what does it mean to say that I "discover" certain thoughts in myself? Since those thoughts, in some form, were already there, am I not really finding out what I already know? The answer, of course, is that, although the thoughts existed, I was not explicitly aware of them. The discovery process involves the conversion of implicit information into explicit information.

For example, some years ago I administered a self-esteem questionnaire to a group of high school students. At the end of the session one young man brought his questionnaire to the front of the room and said, "Sir, that was a real cool questionnaire. I learned a lot from it." What made this comment so interesting was the fact that this anonymous questionnaire *told* him absolutely nothing about himself; it only *asked* him about himself. Whatever knowledge he had about himself when he turned in his questionnaire he had brought with him. Yet he *felt* that he knew more about himself after answering my questions. The increment in knowledge consisted of becoming explicitly aware of certain thoughts about himself that he had implicitly held. This incident is, of course, only an accentuation of experiences that this young man may be experiencing and has been experiencing for years, many times a day.

In the course of social interaction, then, we are bombarded with questions which constantly compel us to conduct a search of our internal mental and emotional events. Some of these may be in the forefront of consciousness, others may be buried in the deeper recesses of the mind. But in either case our attention is directed to an inner world of thought and feeling. Social interaction is thus ceaselessly drawing the individual's attention to this invisible private world.

Communication

Mead (1934) observed:

> I know of no other form of behavior than the linguistic in which the individual is an object to himself, and, so far as I can see, the individual is not a self in the reflexive sense unless he is an object to himself. It is this fact that gives a critical importance to communication, since this is a type of behavior in which the individual does so respond to himself. (p. 142)

Speech, as noted earlier, may either be expressive or instrumental. Among young children, speech tends to be expressive. When young children speak, they do so chiefly for the pleasure of talking, not for the purpose of producing an intended effect on another person's mind. Instrumental speech, on the other hand, is governed by the wish to affect the mind of the listener. When adults speak, they do not simply express what is on their minds. Rather, they fashion messages. Message fashioning radically alters the nature of the communication process. To illustrate, let me take an example that represents—in slow motion, so to speak—the much more rapid series of events that go on within and between speakers.

Assume that I am in the process of writing a professional paper. As my thought are converted into messages, I reflect *in advance* on how my statements will appear to reviewers, given my assumptions about their ways of thought. I may anticipate that they will judge a certain argument to have logical flaws; or I may realize that, although a certain statement is clear to me, it may not be clear to a reader; or I may recognize that they will challenge the methodology used; and so on. In formulating my message, then, I take account of the reactions of the anticipated audience, given my assumptions about their ways of thought. On the basis of these imagined responses, I revise my message in an effort to produce an intended effect on their minds.

Although the preparation of a professional paper can scarcely be considered a typical event in most people's lives, my point is that most or all of these steps occur in the course of ordinary conversation. Say I suddenly turn around and see a young woman I know wearing clothing that strikes me as ludicrous. A thought springs to mind: "My goodness, you look ridiculous." Before speaking, however, I anticipate how my message will strike her. I am fond of her and know she is very sensitive. I may therefore suppress the thought entirely; or I may edit it in an effort to modify its impact. I may, for example, substitute the statement, "My, what an interesting outfit." This simple instance involves all of the same steps or stages as the preparation of the professional paper.

All this, of course, may take place in a matter of seconds or even milliseconds. This is possible, of course, because inner speech is not the same as outer speech. Inner speech is characterized by certain processes of condensation, simplification, and acceleration which make it possible for these stages to be completed with extreme rapidity (Vygotsky 1962). Moreover, different streams of thought may be flowing concurrently along different channels and each may exercise an effect upon the other.

When we carry on a conversation with someone the thought that springs to mind may be decidedly different from the message we verbalize. First we take the role of the other and consider the message from his or her point of view. How will it sound? What effect will it have on our listener's thoughts and, through that, his or her feelings and behaviors? The answers we give to these questions will depend on our assumptions about the listener's information needs, attitudes, values, motives, intentions, or other cognitive components or processes.

In instrumental speech, then, the initiating thought is a rough draft, subject to editing and revision, before it is expressed audibly (or, in many cases, remains unexpressed). The kinds of questions that the individual may direct toward her initiating thought may be: What impact will it have on the listener's mind? Will the listener be enlightened? angered? amused? offended? bored? saddened? How well does this anticipated effect correspond to the one she wishes to produce? If she concludes that the unspoken message that she has tentatively formulated will produce an undesired effect on the listener's mind (and, through that, on his or her behavior), she may re-edit and further revise it, again anticipating the other's probable response to the new version, based on her assumptions about that person's mental content.

This editing and revision process continues even *after* silent thought becomes audible speech. The reason, as Mead (1934) noted, is that people listen to the sound of their own words. Thus, my argument which in the precommunicative stage appeared to me to be so persuasive sounds like a jumble when I hear it verbalized. Anticipating the listener's reaction, I has-ten to rephrase the argument, add examples, define my terms more pre-cisely, and further modify the message in ways better designed to produce their intended mental effects on the listener.

We thus see that the speech act is a multistaged process that demands simultaneous attention to two minds: ego's and alter's. In the course of growing up, we communicate with others tens of thousands of times. In many of these conversations the role-taking processes described above will occur. All this demands constant attention to our communicative inten-tions, message fashioning, editing, revising, rehearsing, and so on. The point I wish to emphasize is that, in each of these steps, *we are focusing our attention on our own thoughts.* To hold our own thoughts before us as objects of our own reflection is to objectify these thoughts. Thought be-comes conscious of itself (James 1890/1950); we come to think of ourselves as thinkers.

A Revolution in Thought. But that is not the end of the matter. There is a further stage: a revolutionary change in human thought that occurs when certain stages of the speech act, becoming habitual, take place in the ab-sence of other people. Even when we are alone we direct our thoughts to our thoughts. Our response to these thoughts, however, is not necessarily from the viewpoint of a specific other (although it may be) but from our own viewpoint. In other words, we respond to our own internal events on the basis of our own system of values, beliefs, standards, modes of reason-ing, moral precepts, and so on. But our own viewpoint, as Mead (1934) made clear, is based on the internalization of the generalized viewpoint of the society as a whole. It is from people in general that we learn that certain ideas are good (tolerance, patriotism) and others bad (prejudice, immoral-ity); that certain ways of thought are logical (syllogistic reasoning) and oth-ers illogical (syncretic reasoning); that certain emotions are good (love, kin-dness), and others bad (anger, jealousy). It is in terms of these and related values and criteria that we come to respond to our own internal thoughts, feelings, and motives. We are, in effect, perceiving our internal events from the perspective of the broader society—the "generalized other" (Mead 1934).

In the course of growing up, then, the individual comes to adopt a "third-party" attitude toward his or her internal events. The upshot is that the mind brings itself under its own surveillance. It comes to pay attention to its own content, monitors itself, responds to itself. Once these processes come fully into play, reflexivity is complete.

When the mind turns its attention to the exploration, examination, and evaluation of its own content, it is clearly revealing its dual character. It is both a thinker and an object thought about. Furthermore, the mind's exploration of its own content has important practical consequences. Although it is not possible to go into these here, the general point can be readily stated: if we don't know what we think, we cannot decide how to act. It is not without reason, then, that the human organism, in contrast to the rest of nature, is so deeply involved in attending to its internal events.

Although it may sound strange to say so, I believe that it is appropriate to view this process as a form of social interaction, to characterize it as "taking the role of the self." People examine their thoughts and feelings, judge them, evaluate them, criticize them, and even create devices to alter them. But when the human mind, exploring its own content, finds itself baffled by its own thoughts, emotions, and behaviors, it is in effect unable to take the role of the self. It is at this stage that it may call into question its own mental status.

How shall one describe this entity that is so busily engaged in observing and acting upon itself? Explicitly or implicitly, most writers appear to postulate the existence of some internal agent that is both observer and regulator of the self. Various terms have been used to refer to this central guiding influence—the observing ego, the agent, the executor. Some philosophers view it as a panoptical scanner, looking inward as well as outward, busily peering into its own nooks and crannies, judging what it has observed, and making decisions about the thoughts it wishes to have. Whether or not one wishes to subscribe to this kind of homuncularism, it is nonetheless clear that the mind is taking an active part in observing itself and in attempting to determine its own content. When the child, to use Piaget's expression, "develops the habit of watching itself think," it experiences a revolution in its own thought processes that will remain with it throughout life.

Mental Disorder

The ability of the human mind to take itself as the object of its own inspection, reflection, and regulation clearly exemplifies the phenomenon of human reflexivity. In this process the essential duality of self (or mind) is starkly revealed. Here we see the mind as subject, actively exploring its world, and there we see the mind as object, as that which is explored and acted upon. As a consequence of human reflexivity, the mind responds to its own thoughts, as it might respond to the thoughts of other persons. It evaluates its own thoughts, judging them to be preposterous, impressed with their cleverness, deploring their vulgarity, appalled at their immorality. The mind even takes a major part in deciding on its own content. By telling itself what to think about and how to think about it, the mind gains some measure of control over its own content (Rosenberg 1990, 1991).

If, by virtue of human reflexivity, the mind can so objectify itself, is it difficult to believe that, in reflecting on its content, it should find itself to be incomprehensible? Not at the moment of experience, of course, but on reflection on it. The assumptions people make about others' mental processes can be applied to their own internal events as well. On reflection, self-objectifying individuals, seeking to understand the operation of their own minds or actions, may nevertheless find themselves at a loss to understand and explain their own inner processes. Where, they ask, did I ever get the strange idea that I could paint? Why did I make such an ass of myself at the party last night? How could I pull such a blunder on the exam? Such questions reflect the fact that human beings can find their own internal mental events to be incomprehensible.

Among the incomprehensible internal events are those TEBs that appear in the standard psychiatric manuals. On reflection, a man may be baffled by the fact that he hears voices that do not exist; that he is driven to steal things that he does not want; that he is terrified to ride in an elevator that he knows to be safe; that he is unable to respond to the normal objects of erotic arousal; that he strikes out in fury at someone he does not even know; and so on. Is it any wonder that people, finding their own thoughts, feelings, or behaviors to be incomprehensible, should call into question their own mental status?

It is important to note that the judgment of incomprehensibility tends to occur *after* the experienced internal event. At the instant of thought, most of what we think usually makes sense to us. It is only after the thought is objectified, held up to the light of our own examination, that it may strike us as senseless. For example, we may experience a strong feeling of hatred toward a stranger on the street. At the moment of experience the feeling makes sense; that person appears to be hateful. Upon reflection, however, we are perplexed. Why in the world should we have such hostile feelings toward a complete stranger? Seeking to understand the internal mental events that are responsible for this reaction, we find ourselves unable to do so. In other words, we cannot understand our own thoughts.

Studies show that recovered schizophrenics rarely complain about being wrongly diagnosed. They almost always agree that they were mentally disturbed. Although a former patient may know that he believed that his feet were nailed to the floor or that his eyelid was broken (Priest and Steinert 1978, p. 170), after recovery these beliefs make no more sense to him than they do to anyone else. When he finds that he is incomprehensible to himself, he may conclude, just as others conclude about him on the same basis, that he was insane.

A Mind That Found Itself

A striking illustration of this phenomenon is to be found in a classic work by a recovered psychotic. Shortly after the turn of the century, Clifford Beers, a young Yale graduate who had become a businessman, suffered a mental breakdown. He was hospitalized for three years, first at a private sanitorium and later in a state mental hospital. Following his recovery, he wrote a book relating his experiences. This work, *A Mind That Found Itself: An Autobiography,* aroused immense public interest (William James, among others, became deeply involved) and launched Beers on his career as founder and leader of the mental hygiene movement in the United States.

Beers's vivid recollections provided an excellent description of how a psychotic perceived the events he was experiencing. At the time, his thoughts made sense to him; yet after his recovery he knew he had been insane. Although doubtlessly influenced by society's judgment, it was also clear that he found his own internal events incomprehensible and, on that basis, judged them to be mentally disordered.

For example, Beers observed a man outside his hospital room placing bars on the windows. As he later recognized, it was to prevent him from injuring himself by jumping out of the window. Beers had attempted suicide and, having some vague notion that suicide was illegal, leaped to the conclusion that he had been placed under arrest, and that the window bars were part of his jail cell. As a result of his suicide attempt, Beers had sustained injuries to his feet and ankles, and the hospital staff applied hot poultices to reduce the swelling. Beers inferred that the police were sweating him in order to elicit a confession, although he had no idea what they wanted him to confess. Because his broken bones required plaster casts, his legs were shaved. Beers equated this procedure with the treatment accorded murderers in certain barbarous countries. Strips of plaster placed on his forehead happened to form a cross, and Beers believed that the purpose was to brand him a criminal.

Beers's delusion of criminality grew into the conviction of even worse (although much more vague) crimes. He was convinced that the newspapers were filled with reports of his terrible misdeeds. When thousands of Yale men passed by the hospital on their way to a football game, he was convinced they were coming to get him for disgracing his alma mater and that they intended to tear him limb from limb.

In speaking of his visitors, Beers (1910, pp. 57–58) reported:

> Relatives and friends frequently called to see me. . . . I spoke to none, not even to my mother and father. For, though they all appeared about as they

used to appear, I was able to detect some slight difference in look or gesture, and this was enough to confirm my belief that they were impersonators, engaged in a conspiracy, not merely to entrap me, but to incriminate those whom they impersonated. It is not strange, then, that I refused to say anything to them, or to permit them to come near me. To have kissed the woman who was my mother, but whom I believed to be a Federal conspirator, would have been an act of betrayal.

Beers's book is filled with many similar examples, but these should suffice to illustrate the point that at the moment of experience people's interpretation of an event makes sense to them. Given the premise that Beers had dishonored Yale and that thousands were coming to punish him, it is understandable that he should have experienced feelings of terror. Given the premise of his unspeakable crimes, it is understandable that he should have interpreted the plaster on his forehead as a brand of infamy. Given the premise that his parents were actually government agents intent on entrapping him, it is understandable that he should have refused to speak to them or have anything to do with them.

Beers's behavior thus made sense at the instant of action. Upon reflection, however, he found them to be incomprehensible. They made no more sense to him than they did to anyone else.

Because of the human capacity for self-reflection, then, I suggest that people can observe their own thoughts, feelings, and behaviors and, upon reflection, conclude that they are incomprehensible. They are just as much at a loss to understand why they feel so inordinately depressed at what they recognize to be a trivial disappointment as why someone else should have such a puzzling reaction. They may be baffled in their effort to understand why they feel so anxious in the absence of objective threat; why they feel so guilty when they have done nothing wrong; why they are so terrified of riding in an elevator; why they feel that people are following them; and so on. All this is possible because, as a consequence of role-taking and communication processes, people are able to objectify their internal events. Baffled by these internal thoughts and feelings, people may come to question their own mental status, and in some cases to conclude that they are in need of treatment. Ultimately, it is role-taking that explains the phenomenon of psychiatric self-referral.

Summary

Because self-referral is the end-product of a long and complex process, it may be helpful to recapitulate the argument of this chapter. It is the ability to take the role of the other, I have suggested, that makes it possible and necessary for the human organism to focus on internal events. Several different processes are involved. First, as children improve their ability to penetrate the interiors of others' minds, they become increasingly aware that other people are striving to gain entry into theirs. This fact calls to their attention the existence of internal thoughts and feelings. In addition, other people, through direct questions or other probes, compel the individual to look inward. Once maturational processes make it possible, children develop the habit of scrutinizing their thoughts, feelings, and wishes.

Second, the communication process, which depends on role-taking, draws the human mind to the attention of itself. As a result of improved role-taking, speech becomes less and less expressive and more and more instrumental. To an increasing extent, speech comes to consist of fashioned or formulated messages. In order to fashion effective messages, people must objectify their thoughts, must hold them up to the light of their own examination, and must revise and edit them for the interpersonal purposes for which they are intended. This process draws the individual's attention to his or her own thoughts. This process continues, however, even when others are not physically present. The upshot of this sequence of events is an ongoing process of mental self-monitoring: searching, exploring, judging, evaluating, criticizing, analyzing, or otherwise responding to these internal events in terms of the logical, moral, or other criteria that have been learned in the course of socialization and maturation.

As a consequence of these processes, the inner world of thought and feeling is no longer simply experienced. It is *objectified;* the individual's thoughts, feelings, and wishes come to be held as objects of his or her inspection, reflection, and manipulation. Just as people attend to and probe the minds of other persons (taking the role of the other), so they attend to and probe their own minds (taking the role of the self). In both cases, failure to understand these internal mental events represents the foundation on which the judgment of mental disorder rests.

The fact that people may classify themselves as mentally ill, then, does not contradict the role-taking theory of mental disorder. The role-taking process, which appears to be dyadic in nature, is replicated within the individual. It is the process of the "observing ego" casting an eye on such internal mental events as thoughts, feelings, or wishes, or on the behavioral manifestations of such internal events, and finding them unfathomable. The social process of role-taking is thus reproduced internally.

Whether classifying others or themselves as mentally disordered, then, the fundamental process that humans engage in is that of role-taking. When role-taking failure occurs, therefore, it is a source of puzzlement to people. It is in response to the felt need for an explanation of the puzzle that the concept of mental disorder develops.

6
The Mystery of Mental Illness

I nsanity has long been, and continues to be, puzzling and mysterious. There are at least two indications that this is so. First, throughout history, society's reaction to insanity has been strangely inconsistent and contradictory, an ambivalence that persists to this day. Second, contemporary studies of public attitudes find that the phenomenon of insanity continues to be viewed as mysterious, strange, and baffling (Nunnally 1961).

In this chapter I shall argue that the reason for the confusion lies in the nature of the role-taking process. It is the phenomenon of the unread mind that holds the key to the mystery of mental disorder.

Moral Status of Insanity

At the outset of this work I pointed out that at times the insane have been whipped, chained, tortured, exiled, burned at the stake, and subjected to various other horrible forms of punishment. Yet at other times—or even at the same time—the insane have been supported, helped, cared for, nurtured, and provided with various kinds of humane and benign treatment. It is apparent that society has never quite known what to do with the insane— whether to condemn and punish them or to help and support them. Sometimes it has done the first, sometimes the second, and sometimes both simultaneously.

Why this inconsistent and contradictory response of society to insanity? One of the chief reasons, I suggest, lies in the *ambiguous moral status* of mental illness. The meaning of the term "moral status" can be conveyed by comparing crime, on the one hand, with physical illness, on the other. Although there are exceptions, crime is generally considered *bad*. The usual reaction to criminal behavior is to abhor, condemn, and punish it. The reaction to physical illness is quite different. The sick person is much more likely to elicit our sympathy than our condemnation.

But what is the *moral status* of insanity? Is the insane TEB morally reprehensible, and thus deserving of punishment, or morally neutral, and thus deserving of support? This is one source of the uncertainty surrounding the phenomenon of insanity.

For example, when John Hinckley shot President Ronald Reagan, there

99

were widespread feelings of shock and outrage at this appalling act. Many people passionately advocated the imposition of severe punishment. At the same time there were those who felt that Hinckley was the unfortunate victim of a mental illness and that it was society's responsibility to help him.

Or take the notorious case of the "Son of Sam." Over a period of several months, a young man went around New York City searching for young couples necking in automobiles and proceeded to shoot them. In his communications with the press, this young man identified himself as the killer, calling himself the "Son of Sam." As the shootings continued, public outrage grew, passionate denunciations of the killer were voiced, and calls for the most severe punishment were heard. When the perpetrator was finally apprehended, the desire for retribution reached new heights. At the same time there were also those who felt that this young man, who claimed to have committed the murders on the instructions of his neighbor's dog, named Sam, needed and deserved help. Finally, there were those—perhaps the majority—whose feelings about the case were mixed, confused, and contradictory.

It might seem that such bizarre and highly publicized cases tell us little about insanity in general. But the moral status of an act is relevant in less dramatic instances as well. For example, one of Bleuler's patients laughed with delight when she received a printed announcement of her brother's death because she was so pleased by the black borders surrounding the announcement, but she had no emotional reaction to his death. Is this heartless behavior immoral? What about the case of a peeping Tom discovered peering through windows, or a psychosexual deviate who is only able to gain erotic arousal by exposing his genitals in public? Are these people to be pitied for their illness or censured for their immorality? One reason for society's inconsistent and contradictory attitudes and behavior toward the mentally ill lies in the frequent moral ambiguity of insane behavior.

What is it about psychotic behavior that makes us so uncertain about its moral status? The answer is that the moral status of an act depends not so much on the nature of the act itself as on the mental events underlying it. If I hurt a child by suddenly yanking it out of the path of a speeding car, the moral status of the act, and hence the societal reaction to it, depends on the intention imputed to me. If it is believed that my purpose was to hurt the child, I may be upbraided, condemned, and reviled. But if it is believed that my objective was to save the child's life, then I may be lauded, rewarded, and admired. Society's response to my behavior does not so much depend on what I did as on why I did it.

Even the legal system, which generally prefers to focus on behavior rather than intention, nevertheless recognizes that in many—perhaps most—cases the legal status of the act depends on internal mental events. For example, if a person kills someone intentionally, this act is called murder. But if the death was accidental, it is called involuntary manslaughter.

The identical act thus elicits radically different responses, depending on whether the cause is attributed to internal (intentional) or external (accidental) factors.

To identify the moral responsibility of deviant acts, then, people must attempt to probe the actor's intentions, perceptions, motives, definitions of the situation, and so on. The moral status of the act depends on the results of entry into the internal world of actors. That is precisely why the moral status of insane acts is so often ambiguous, why in some instances the act is morally deplored whereas in others it is morally lauded. I contend that the defining feature of madness is role-taking failure. If we cannot understand what is going on in people's minds, we do not know whether to condemn and punish them or absolve them of responsibility. Mental illness thus remains a mysterious phenomenon, a phenomenon whose moral status remains clouded in doubt. It is no wonder that throughout history and across societies the reactions to the insane have been so contradictory and inconsistent and that they remain so today.

Meaning

In his discussion of the methodology of the social sciences, Max Weber (1949) asked, What is it that distinguishes social from physical science? The key difference, he contended, lay in the question of *meaning*. Objective facts of social scientific interest reflected the internal mental events of actors.

Meaning, in this view, does not reside in words or behavior; it resides in thought. One well-known expression of this idea is Mead's (1934) concept of the "significant symbol." To take his example, when someone shakes a fist in your face, you assume he or she has some idea behind it. The meaning of the act is the idea imputed to the actor. If someone shoves you in a crowd, the meaning of the behavior lies in its intent—whether you believe the act was a result of accident or of hostility.

It is for this reason that people do not respond to what others say or do; they respond to what others mean, or to what they believe they mean (Lazarsfeld 1972, Chapter 8). Consider our responses to people's words: if someone says "Call me a taxi," we do not respond by saying "You're a taxi." The same is true of behavior. If someone takes our coat from a rack, the meaning of the act depends on whether his intent was to steal it or whether he has simply mistaken the coat for his own.

Concern with meaning is an adult cognitive process. Young children have poorly developed role-taking skills, and so are largely oblivious to the internal mental events of others. Hence, they tend to respond to words or acts in terms of their visible consequences, not their internal intentions. Consider the following example drawn from Piaget's (1948) studies of moral development: Piaget asked his young subjects to consider two stories. In one, a child is attempting to extract a cookie from a jar that she has been forbidden to touch. In the process she knocks over and breaks a cup. In the other, a child is helping her mother set the table and accidentally knocks over a tray of cups, breaking twelve. Which child deserves the greater punishment? The young child says that the one who broke the larger number of cups deserves the greater punishment. ("For the first child, one slap; for the second child, two slaps.") To the young child the meaning of the act lies in its visible consequences, not in its subjective intent. Although adults are not indifferent to overt consequences, to the adult the meaning of the act basically lies in the internal mental events of the actor.

Role-taking theory thus helps us understand why insane behavior is, in a fundamental sense, meaningless. For example, what are we to make of the words of a Bleuler patient who for years goes around saying "Maybe we should apply court plaster"? What thoughts (motives, purposes, intentions) should we attribute to another patient who spends his days tapping a saliva-moistened finger against the wall? Usually we find it meaningless. It is difficult to overestimate the importance of this fact for social life. If one were somehow to be cut off from the minds of other people, words and behavior would be literally meaningless. It is perhaps this essential meaninglessness of insane behavior that makes it so perplexing, confusing, and mystifying.

Attributional Uncertainty

Whether a given thought, emotion, or behavior is sane or insane is a question that is often clouded in doubt and uncertainty. There are a number of reasons why this is so.

First, as noted earlier, role-taking is basically an *inferential* process. In the final analysis, no human being can ever gain complete entry into the mind of another. The thoughts that we impute to others depend largely on guesses, plausible inferences, sometimes questionable assumptions. This is a lesson that is not lost on people. Experience teaches us that in taking the role of the other there is a distinct possibility that we may be wrong. Others' intentions are misunderstood; their viewpoints are misjudged; the information that we attribute to them turns out to be in error. Hence, the inferences that we draw about other people's internal mental and emotional events are tentative, readily subject to modification and revision. Since the attribution of insanity depends on role-taking failure, our uncertainty about the mental status of a TEB is simply an extension of the general uncertainty that is part and parcel of the role-taking process.

A second reason for the uncertainty surrounding the attribution of insanity is our doubt about the existence of a *social consensus*. The judgment of insanity, as noted earlier, is based not only on one's inability to read the other's thoughts, but also on the assumption that *most people* in society would also find these thoughts incomprehensible. But this assumption must rest on reading the mind of society, or, in Mead's (1934) terms, the "generalized other." People recognize that behavior that seems crazy to them may not be viewed that way by other people. But if we are *not sure* how most people in the society would respond to a given TEB, then we may remain in a state of uncertainty about the mental status of the act.

Third, it is often unclear whether the cause of the role-taking failure lies in the self or in the other. Is our inability to grasp the other's viewpoint attributable to our own limitations, or is the other person incomprehensible? We know that it may be our own ignorance of the actor's biography, the nature of the situation, the other's underlying motives, and so on that is responsible for our failure to understand the other's words or acts. People may thus be uncertain about the mental status of a TEB because of the inherent uncertainty of the role-taking process.

It is for these reasons that the attribution of insanity tends to be characterized by so much doubt, uncertainty, and perplexity. Faced with words or actions that seriously defy their understanding, people may scramble about frantically in search of an hypothesis that accounts for the actor's thoughts, feelings, or behaviors. People's initial response in the face of role-taking failure is to suspend judgment about the mental status of the act pending further information or clarification. The attribution of insanity is thus not made lightly or quickly, but slowly, reluctantly, and as a last resort. In other words, the incomprehensibility of a TEB must be quite extreme before people will confidently conclude that it is insane.

Yarrow et al.'s (1955) research on the wives of schizophrenics illustrates this point. They found that wives' initial response to husbands' schizophrenic behavior was to attempt to "normalize" it. Confronted with thoughts, emotions, and behaviors that defied their understanding, these women worked hard to place these TEBs within a framework that made sense to them. When the first symptoms appeared, they rarely interpreted their husbands' behavior as insane. Initially, the husband might describe his physical problems, complaints, or worries; might deviate from normal routines of behavior; might appear nervous, irritable, or worried; might show changes or accentuations of personality traits; might exhibit verbal or physical withdrawal; might show aggressive, assaultive, or suicidal behavior; might describe strange or bizarre thoughts, delusions, or hallucinations; and so on. Almost invariably the wife tried to fit the behavior into some causal or motivational theory that made sense to her. In some cases she might see it as a character problem (he is "spoiled" or "lazy" or "weak"); in other cases as a bad habit (he drinks too much); in still others as an understandable response to internal or external stress (he stayed home from work because he just didn't feel good).

Although the wives found the behavior extremely puzzling, they almost never first interpreted it as insanity. Typically, they attempted to understand the behavior according to their implicit theories of personality, motivation, and so on. It was only when they could no longer explain the behavior in terms of any situational or dispositional theories that made sense to them that they finally came to question the mental status of their husbands. In other words, they began to suspect their husbands' sanity when they were certain that they could not comprehend their husbands' mental events, that the incomprehensibility did not stem from their own lack of knowledge, and that most other people in the society would also find such behavior incomprehensible. For these women, the entire experience was filled with doubt, bewilderment, and confusion.

Insanity as Illness

The confusion and mystery that so often surrounds insanity is due to society's misidentification of the locus of the problem. Implicit in almost all of the writings on insanity is the assumption that the problem resides within the individual. To be sure, external forces (e.g., demons in the middle ages, family interaction today) may be seen as the causes of the problem, but the problem itself is ultimately believed to lie within the victim. It is he who speaks and acts so strangely, he who requires treatment. We can thus see why efforts to understand insanity have focused on understanding the insane.

But if one focuses upon the insane person, then one can only gain a limited understanding of the problem. The reason is that mental illness is not simply an *intrapersonal* phenomenon; it is also an *interpersonal* process. It takes two to make a psychotic: an actor and an observer. Insanity, then, is a social problem, not an individual one.

The location of insanity within the individual finds its clearest expression in the medical conception of insanity as an illness. Psychiatry is a branch of medicine. The mentally ill are treated by doctors in offices, hospitals, or other medical settings. Institutions formerly labeled "lunatic asylums" are now called "mental hospitals." The psychotic is considered sick.

But mental illness is not an illness like any other. Although biological factors may play a causal role in both mental and physical illness, mental illness involves a number of social factors that are largely irrelevant to physical illness.

The difference is evident when one considers the bearing of social contexts, structural conditions, cultural variability, and other social influences on the meaning of symptoms. Medicine generally assumes that the essential nature of a disease is independent of such social influences. A heart attack is a heart attack whether the victim is upper, middle, or lower class; black or white; Hispanic or Anglo. It is the same whether it occurs in a church, a bookstore, or a sports stadium; in a large city or a small town; while painting pictures or playing cards. In other words, the physical disorder has nothing to do with when, where, or to whom it occurs.

This is not true of mental disorder. For example, the mental status of a TEB may depend on the social identity of the actor. The DSM–III–R Casebook (CB, pp. 182–83) reports the case of a woman who, over the course of the previous three or four years, had stolen several blouses, a couple of sweaters, and a skirt from some shops. What made this behavior so strange was that her husband's income exceeded a quarter of a million dollars annually and that their investments were even larger. Furthermore, she often stole clothes that she did not really like and had no desire to wear. After the event, she tended to feel anxious and guilty because of what she had done. The psychiatrist had no difficulty in diagnosing this behavior as kleptomania. Yet the identical act by a welfare recipient would be considered entirely sane. The behavior in itself, then, is not a symptom of mental disorder. In this case, it depends on the social identity of the actor.

The same is true of other contexts and situations. In general, a physical symptom means the same thing no matter what the context or situation. For example, the symptoms of renal failure are the same whether they appear at home, at work, or on the street. Mental symptoms, in contrast, may depend on the context as much as on the behavior. For example, nudity on the street has an entirely different mental status than nudity in the home or in a nudist colony. Singing during a college lecture is not the same as singing during choir practice. Uncontrolled laughter at a funeral is not the same as uncontrolled laughter at a comedy. It is evident that mental illness, unlike physical illness, cannot be understood solely by reference to intrapersonal processes. Social and interpersonal processes thoroughly permeate the phenomenon.

In sum, people are confused by insanity because they think of it as anchored solely within the individual. But the problem also resides within society, often involving, for example, legal, moral, and interpersonal issues. Legal issues are interwoven with psychological ones in kleptomania, pyromania, and antisocial personality disorder. Moral considerations are part and parcel of such psychosexual deviations as exhibitionism, pedophilia, and voyeurism. Interpersonal relations are almost always damaged by schizophrenia. Although bodily processes may cause certain mentally disordered TEBs, mental disorder is essentially a social, not a biological, phenomenon. When the courts decide whether or not an individual has the right to dispose of his or her property as he or she wishes; when people are apprehended by the police for public display of nudity; when people steal or lie without reason; when others look upon the actor as strange or bizarre—these are matters of social definition, not biological dysfunction. When one judges a person to be mentally ill, as Szasz (1987) points out, one is more likely to do so on the basis of social, legal, and ethical criteria than on the basis of biological ones.

The role-taking approach, it should be noted, does not deny that the mentally ill may indeed be afflicted with certain physical or biochemical abnormalities. Role-taking theory takes no position regarding the causes of the symptoms of mental disorder. These may be genetic, biochemical, intrauterine, interpersonal, cultural, social structural, or any other. The role-taking position is that whatever it is that is responsible for producing those TEBs that are symptomatic of mental illness, the reason they are so classified in that they represent role-taking failure on the part of the observer. I thus suggest that when people look within the individual in an effort to understand mental illness, they may end up perplexed because they are to a large extent looking in the wrong place.

In sum, I suggest that it is for these reasons that, throughout history and across societies, insanity has always struck people as a puzzling and mysterious phenomenon. People have not known what to make of it, how to identify it, or what to do about it. Hence, society's treatment of the insane traditionally has been, and continues to be, inconsistent and contradictory.

Role-taking theory, I suggest, helps us to unravel the mystery. The problem of insanity proves to be the problem of the unread mind. It is not possible to understand insanity without reference to one of the most fundamental of all social processes—the process whereby people strive to gain entry into the ultimately inaccessible internal worlds of other human beings.

But role-taking theory can contribute to our understanding of mental illness in other ways as well. First, it sheds light on the milder mental disorders as well as the more serious ones emphasized in this work. Second, it provides insight into the purposes of psychotherapy. Finally, it has an important bearing on the future prospects for a cross-cultural psychiatry. Let me describe each of these contributions.

Severity of Mental Disorder

Throughout this work the focus has been on the more serious manifestations of mental disorder, those that we associate with such terms as psychosis, insanity, or madness. But what about the milder disorders, such as the personality disorders or those symptoms of depression or anxiety that used to be called neuroses? Does role-taking theory have anything to tell us about these psychological problems?

One approach to this question is to think of mental disorder as a continuum, ranging from complete madness at one end to complete sanity at the other. Role-taking may also be thought of as a continuum, from complete success to complete failure. It is thus possible to see how the severity of mental disorder corresponds to the degree of role-taking success and failure.

The more serious disorders are those closest to the experience of role-taking failure (incomprehensible); the less serious, closer to the experience of role-taking success (comprehensible). To cite an example from DSM–III–R (p. 404), ". . . a depressed person who underestimates his achievements would not be described as psychotic, whereas one who believes he has caused a natural catastrophe would be so described." In other words, the latter belief strikes us as more incomprehensible that the former; hence, it is judged to be a more serious symptom.

Because role-taking success or failure is a matter of degree, many instances of mental disorder appear to be characterized by partial understanding and partial incomprehensibility. For example, at first glance, much of the manic's behavior seems to be comprehensible. A wish to be with people, to talk to them, to tell them plans and ideas, does not defy our understanding. What perplexes us, however, is why the manic wakes us up at three in the morning to do so. His or her behavior is thus both understandable and at the same time bewildering. Similarly, the manic may be open-handed and generous. There is nothing puzzling about that. But we become mystified when he walks into a bar where he knows no one and orders drinks for all the customers; or gives the entire contents of her wallet to a panhandler.

Our reactions to somatoform disorders also show the same ambivalence. We have no difficulty in understanding why a man who constantly complains of illness goes from one doctor to another in search of a cure. But when the search goes on year after year, resulting in a shelf full of pills and a number of unnecessary operations—all without the slightest evidence of a physical disorder—we become perplexed by the behavior. We experience partial understanding, partial bafflement.

Now compare these cases with that of a schizophrenic ("Emilio"), who is brought to the hospital for treatment (CB, p. 137). He arrives wearing bedroom slippers, a baseball cap, and a worn overcoat. A variety of medals hang around his neck. He walks with a mincing step, conspicuously swinging his hips. In response to the question of what he has been doing since his last hospitalization, he replies that he has been "eating wires and setting fires." The remainder of the interview continues in the same vein.

The difference between the schizophrenic and the others is that it is almost impossible to glean the internal mental events that underlie the schizophrenic's behavior. One reason that it is considered a more severe mental disorder, then, is the fact that it is almost totally, rather than partially, incomprehensible.

This view of mental disorder as a continuum of role-taking success or failure also sheds light on a question that is rarely addressed in the literature, namely, What is meant by "sanity"? This question is rarely raised because medicine focuses so overwhelmingly on illness, not on health. Although lip service is sometimes paid to the importance of "wellness," by and large health is simply the "absence of illness," or, at best, the ability to forestall or resist illness.

To be sure, this is less true in the psychological realm, where there is interest in "positive mental health" (Jahoda 1958; Maslow 1971) and "psychological well-being" (Mirowsky and Ross 1989). Nevertheless, psychiatry generally pays little attention to sanity, and tends to view it as a residual category. If someone is not insane, then he or she is sane.

Role-taking theory suggests that sanity is not simply the absence of insanity. On the contrary, the attribution of sanity is a positive affirmation of role-taking success. If I call a man sane, I am saying that his internal mental events make sense to me. Sanity, then, is not simply a residual category; it is an interpersonal process.

Therapeutic Implications

Given the radical difference between the role-taking and psychiatric approaches, one might think that role-taking theorists would be out of sympathy with most of the current psychotherapeutic procedures. But that is not the case. Role-taking theory does not speak to the question of *how* therapy is conducted, but to *why* therapy is conducted, and how its effectiveness is assessed.

The range and variety of therapies currently available boggles the mind. Parloff (1984) estimated that there were at least 250 "brands" of therapy on the market. These therapies, according to Klerman (1982), fall into four general categories.

1. Most psychotherapies are based on verbal dialogues. These include psychoanalysis, client-centered therapy, insight therapy, encounter groups, rational-emotive therapy, transactional analysis, and various kinds of behavior therapy and group therapy.

2. A second class of therapies also depend on verbal processes but represent more unusual or dramatic procedures, "often combined with specific behavioral methods of rehearsal or with altered states of consciousness" (Klerman 1982, p. 185), such as psychodrama, gestalt therapy, progressive desensitization, implosive therapy, operant conditioning, and hypnosis.

3. A third class of therapies are those designed to affect bodily processes or experience, such as aversion therapies, biofeedback, bioenergetic therapy, and rolfing.

4. Finally, a wide variety of psychopharmacologic agents, such as antidepressant and antipsychotic drugs, as well as physical interventions like electroconvulsive therapy, are used in the treatment of mental disorders. Some of these drugs, incidentally, are among the most widely used medications in the Western world.

The question is, What are these therapies designed to accomplish? Although their objectives vary widely, I believe there is one objective they all share: to eliminate those TEBs that other people cannot understand and to replace then with TEBs that they can. Therapists, although they are not aware of it, are often engaged in efforts to make patients more comprehensible to nonpatients.

There is, then, no necessary inconsistency between role-taking theory and current psychiatric practice. Role-taking theory agrees that whatever therapies—verbal, psychopharmacologic, physical—can effect desired change are to be encouraged and supported. What role-taking theory contributes is an understanding of one of the important purposes of therapy, namely, *to change the patient in such a way that other people can grasp what is going on in his or her mind.*

If this is so, then it suggests that investigators might be well-advised to consider another, very different, criterion for assessing the effectiveness of therapy. This could be to learn whether, as the therapy progresses, *other people* who interact regularly with the patient come to find his or her words and actions to be less baffling. An extension of this idea would be to examine whether certain common consequences of role-taking failure, such as marital dissolution, employment problems, and loss of friends, are altered as a result of therapeutic interventions. The effort to assess therapeutic effectiveness by studying other people's reactions to the patient would be in keeping with the conception of insanity as role-taking failure.

Cross-Cultural Psychiatry

A major area of interest in the sociology of mental disorder is the effect of culture on psychological disorder. By culture we refer to the norms, practices, values, characteristic ways of thought, and so on that prevail in a society. Although subcultural variations are to be found within large, heterogeneous, complex societies, there are distinct limits to our ability to understand the impact of culture on mental disorder within a single society. An adequate understanding of this question demands comparisons across cultures.

The World Health Organization (WHO) collects statistics on health and illness throughout the world. The fundamental assumption is that the same diagnoses refer to the same medical phenomena. A heart attack, for example, is independent of national identity, cultural practices, economic systems, and social constructions of reality. Although conceptions of the nature and causes of physical illness may vary widely, it is nevertheless assumed that the essential nature of the illness is the same in different societies.

It is also assumed that the signs and symptoms of the diseases—the diagnostic indicators—are the same. However varied societies may be, chest pains, electrocardiogram abnormalities, angiogram recordings, and so on are assumed to have the same coronary significance. Hence, the WHO can collect statistics on the incidence and prevalence of physical illnesses throughout the world with reasonable confidence that they are dealing with the same biological phenomena.

When it comes to mental illness, however, that may not be the case. The thoughts, emotions, and behaviors that are insane in one society may be sane in another. This point has been stressed by the cultural relativists. According to Weckowicz (1984, p. 169):

> Ruth Benedict . . . was perhaps the most vocal member of this point of view. According to her a normal member of the Zuni tribe would be diagnosed as suffering from obsessional-compulsive neurosis by a Western psychiatrist. The typical behavior of Dobu islanders would be adjudged as paranoid by the Western standards. A shaman hearing voices of spirits would be labeled a schizophrenic. The same would apply to St. Joan of Arc if she were transplanted from the Middle Ages to the modern Western world.

It is unquestionably true that certain mental syndromes that appear in one culture may not be found in another (Eaton 1980, pp. 28–29). The *koro* syndrome in China is a fear that the penis is shrinking into the abdomen. *Latah,* a syndrome found in several cultures, occurs among women who have been frightened suddenly and who behave as though they were hypnotized, automatically obeying every command. In Malaysia, the syndrome of *Amok* is found. It involves a sudden outbreak of destructive and violent behavior—behavior that the victim cannot remember after the event. Other distinctive syndromes have been reported in other societies.

Some writers (e.g., Eaton and Weil 1955) have questioned whether the phenomenon of insanity or psychosis as we understand it in the West is even to be found in smaller, more homogeneous, more traditional societies. This question has been carefully examined by Jane Murphy (1982) in her studies of mental illness in two widely separated societies; a tribe of Yupik-speaking Eskimos in the Bering Sea just below the Arctic Circle and a tribe of Egba Yorubas of Nigeria, a tropical area near the equator. The Eskimos are a hunting-and-gathering society, whereas the Yorubas live in settled agricultural villages.

Is the concept of insanity as we understand it recognized in these societies? First, Murphy notes, both languages include terms that correspond essentially to our meaning of "crazy." Among the Eskimo, this term is *nuthkavihak.* She writes (p. 54):

> Descriptions of how *nuthkavihak* is manifest include such phenomena as "talking to oneself," "screaming at somebody who does not exist," "believing that a child or husband was murdered by witchcraft when nobody else believes it," "believing oneself to be an animal," "refusing to eat for fear

that it will kill the person," "running away," "getting lost," "hiding in strange places," "making strange grimaces," "drinking urine," "becoming strong and violent," "killing dogs," "threatening people."

The Yoruba language also contains a word, *were,* which means insanity. *Were* is manifested in such behavior as hearing voices, laughing without reason, speaking incessantly, making piles of sticks with no purpose, removing one's clothes in public, defecating in public, suddenly hitting someone without reason, and so on.

Several points are worth noting. First, in both societies a term that corresponds closely to the Western conception of insanity is clearly recognized. Second, this concept, as in the West, is clearly distinguished from crime, immorality, and other forms of deviance on the one hand and physical illness on the other. Both the Eskimos and the Yorubas have words for lying, cheating, theft, and so on; this behavior is recognized as distinctly different from *nuthkavihak* and *were* and is condemned and punished. *Nuthkavihak* and *were,* in contrast, tend to elicit sympathy from members of the tribe, and efforts are made to help the victims through the ministrations of shamans and healers. These disorders are also clearly distinguished from physical illnesses; the problem is recognized to be located in the mind, not in the body.

Other anthropologists report similar findings. On the basis of such reports, Weckowicz (1984, p. 173) goes so far as to claim that "all cultures have the concept of madness" (see also Eaton 1980, pp. 29–30; Murphy 1982). To be sure, the content of insane TEBs will vary from society to society. A psychotic in a traditional isolated society will not identify himself as Napoleon, Alexander the Great, or even Elvis Presley. Conceptions of the causes of the mental illness are also likely to differ in the different societies, for example, demon possession among the Eskimos and Yoruba, the Oedipus complex in the West. The therapies will also differ: in traditional societies, the therapy may be based on the incantations of shamans and healers; in our society, on phenothiazines and tricyclic antidepressants. Yet despite these and other differences, the essential nature of psychosis appears to be much the same throughout the world.

How can one explain this similarity? The chief reason, I suggest, is the fact that role-taking is a cultural universal, and that the fundamental ways of thought and patterns of communication are much the same everywhere: false beliefs about external reality that are not held by others and for which no persuasive evidence can be adduced; speech patterns (e.g., flight of ideas, incoherence, neologisms, perseveration) that communicate no information and in which the line of reasoning cannot be discerned; sensory experiences that appear in the absence of external stimuli (except where these are socially shared or role-related); behavior characterized by an absence of purpose; the apparent lack of free will; the loss of a sense of self and identity; patterns of social withdrawal and interpersonal estrangement—all these and similar TEBs will be found to be incomprehensible by people in all societies. In other words, these ways of thought will tend to produce role-taking failure whenever they occur. Furthermore, members of different societies will assume that not only they, but also most of the other people in their society, would be unable to take the role of the actor exhibiting these TEBs.

Despite major differences in the content of thought across cultures, then, comparison of rates of mental disorder in different societies and the study of the social influences bearing on these disorders are meaningful and feasible. The reason is that in all societies role-taking is an essential feature of the social process. It is when role-taking fails that the individual's mental status is called into question. Ultimately, madness is attributed to people whose internal mental events other people cannot read.

References

American Psychiatric Association. 1980. *Diagnostic and Statistical Manual of Mental Disorders*. Third Edition. Washington, DC: American Psychiatric Association.

———. 1987. *Diagnostic and Statistical Manual of Mental Disorders*. Third Edition, Revised. Washington, DC: American Psychiatric Association.

Asch, Solomon E. 1946. "Forming Impressions of Personality." *Journal of Abnormal and Social Psychology* 41:258–290.

Averill, James. 1980. "Emotion and Anxiety: Sociocultural, Biological, and Psychological Determinants." In *Explaining Emotions*, edited by A.O. Rorty, 37–72. Berkeley: University of California Press.

Becker, Howard S. 1963. *Outsiders: Studies in the Sociology of Deviance*. New York: Free Press.

Beers, Clifford W. 1910. *A Mind That Found Itself: An Autobiography*. Second Edition. New York: Longmans, Green, and Co.

Bleuler, Eugen. 1911/1950. *Dementia Praecox or the Group of Schizophrenias*. Translated by Joseph Zinkin. New York: International Universities Press.

Blumer, Herbert. 1969. *Symbolic Interactionism: Perspective and Method*. Englewood Cliffs, NJ: Prentice-Hall.

Bord, Richard J. 1971. "Rejection of the Mentally Ill: Continuities and Further Developments." *Social Problems* 18:496–509.

Broughton, John M. 1978. "The Development of Concepts of Self, Mind, Reality, and Knowledge." In *Social Cognition: New Directions for Child Development* (No. 1). San Francisco: Jossey-Bass.

Campbell, Robert J. 1981. *Psychiatric Dictionary*. Fifth Edition. New York: Oxford University Press.

Cockerham, William C. 1989. *Sociology of Mental Disorder*. Second Edition. Englewood Cliffs, NJ: Prentice-Hall.

Cooley, Charles H. 1902. *Human Nature and the Social Order*. New York: Scribners.

Damon, William, and Daniel Hart. 1988. *Self-Understanding in Childhood and Adolescence*. Cambridge: Cambridge University Press.

Deutsch, Albert. 1949. *The Mentally Ill in America: A History of Their Care and Treatment from Colonial Times*. New York: Columbia University Press.

Dohrenwend, Bruce P., and Barbara S. Dohrenwend. 1969. *Social Status and Psychological Disorder*. New York: Wiley.

Durkheim, Emile. 1964. *The Division of Labor in Society*. New York: Free Press.

Eaton, J.W., and R.J. Weil. 1955. *Culture and Mental Disorders*. Glencoe, Il: Free Press.

Eaton, William W. 1980. *The Sociology of Mental Disorder*. New York: Praeger.

Erikson, Kai. 1962. "Notes on the Sociology of Deviance." *Social Problems* 9:307–314.

Fingarette, Herbert. 1972. *The Meaning of Criminal Insanity.* Berkeley: University of California Press.

Flavell, John H. 1970. "Concept Development." In *Carmichael's Manual of Child Psychology*, vol. 1, edited by P.H. Mussen. New York: Wiley.

———. 1974. "The Development of Inferences About Others." In *Understanding Other Persons*, edited by T. Mischel, 66–116. Oxford: Blackwell.

Flavell, John H., in collaboration with Patricia Botkin, Charles Fry, John Wright, and Paul Jarvis. 1968. *The Development of Role-Taking and Communication Skills in Children.* New York: Wiley.

Foucault, Michel. 1973. *Madness and Civilization: A History of Insanity in the Age of Reason.* New York: Random House.

Gallatin, Judith. 1982. *Abnormal Psychology: Concepts, Issues, Trends.* New York: Macmillan.

Gallup, Gordon G., and Susan D. Suarez. 1986. "Self-Awareness and the Emergence of Mind in Humans and Other Primates." In *Psychological Perspectives on the Self*, vol. 3, edited by J. Suls and A.G. Greenwald, 3–26. Hillsdale, NJ: Lawrence Erlbaum.

Gibbs, Jack P. 1990. "The Sociology of Deviance and Social Control." In *Social Psychology: Sociological Perspectives.* Transaction Edition. Edited by M. Rosenberg and R. H. Turner, 483–522. New Brunswick, NJ: Transaction Books.

Goffman, Erving. 1955. "On Face-Work: An Analysis of Ritual Elements in Social Interaction." *Psychiatry* 18:213–231.

———. 1963. *Stigma: Notes on the Management of Spoiled Identity.* Englewood Cliffs, NJ: Prentice-Hall

Gottesman, Irving, and James Shields. 1972. *Schizophrenia and Genetics: A Twin Study Vantage Point.* New York: Academic Press.

Gove, Walter R. 1970. "Societal Reaction as an Explanation of Mental Illness: An Evaluation." *American Sociological Review 35:873–884.*

———. *(ed). 1980. Labeling Deviant Behavior.* Beverly Hills, CA.: Sage.

———. 1982. "The Current Status of the Labeling Theory of Mental Illness." In *Deviance and Mental Illness*, edited by W.R. Gove, 273–300. Beverly Hills, CA: Sage.

Halpert, Harold P. 1970. "Public Opinion and Attitudes About Mental Health." In *Social Psychology and Mental Health*, edited by H. Wechsler, L. Solomon, and B.M. Kramer, 489–504. New York: Holt, Rinehart and Winston.

Hamburg, David A., George V. Coelho, and John E. Adams. 1974. "Coping and Adaptation: Steps Toward a Synthesis of Biological and Social Perspectives." In *Coping and Adaptation*, edited by G. Coelho, D. Hamburg, and J. Adams, 403–440. New York: Basic Books.

Harre, Rom. 1986. "An Outline of the Social Constructionist Viewpoint." In *The Social Construction of Emotions*, edited by R. Harre, 2–14. Oxford: Blackwell.

Hartley, Eugene L., and Ruth E. Hartley. 1952. *Fundamentals of Social Psychology.* New York: Knopf.

Heider, Fritz. 1958. *The Psychology of Interpersonal Relations.* New York: Wiley.

Heiss, Jerold. 1981. *The Social Psychology of Interaction.* Englewood Cliffs, NJ: Prentice-Hall.

Hewitt, John P. 1990. *Self and Society: A Symbolic Interactionist Social Psychology.* Fifth Edition. Needham Heights, MA: Allyn and Bacon.

Hewitt, John P., and Randall G. Stokes. 1975. "Disclaimers." *American Sociological Review* 40:1–11.

Hobbes, Thomas. 1968. *Leviathan.* New York: Penguin.

Jahoda, Marie. 1958. *Current Concepts of Positive Mental Health.* New York: Basic Books.

James, William. 1890/1950. *The Principles of Psychology.* New York: Dover.

Jourard, Sidney. 1964. *The Transparent Self.* Princeton, NJ: Van Nostrand.

Kagan, Jerome. 1981. *The Second Year of Life.* Cambridge, MA: Harvard University.

Keller, A., L. Ford, and J. Meacham. 1978. "Development of Self-Concept in Preschool Children." *Developmental Psychology* 14:483–489.

Kelley, Harold H. 1967. "Attribution Theory in Social Psychology." In *Nebraska Symposium on Motivation*, edited by D. Levine, 192–238. Lincoln, NE: University of Nebraska Press.

Kety, Seymour. 1975. "Biochemistry of the Major Psychoses." In *Comprehensive Textbook of Psychiatry.* Second Edition. Edited by A. Freedman, H. Kaplan, and B. Sadock, 178–187. Baltimore: Williams and Wilkins.

Klerman, Gerald L. 1982. "The Psychiatric Revolution of the Past Twenty-Five Years." In *Deviance and Mental Illness,* edited by W.R. Gove, 177–198. Beverly Hills, CA: Sage.

Kohlberg, Lawrence. 1976. "Moral Stages and Moralization: The Cognitive-Developmental Approach." In *Moral Development and Behavior,* edited by T. Lickona. New York: Holt, Rinehart and Winston.

Kohn, Melvin L. 1972. "Class, Family, and Schizophrenia: A Reformulation." *Social Forces* 50:295–304.

———. 1974. "Social Class and Schizophrenia: A Critical Review and Reformulation." In *Explorations in Psychiatric Sociology*, edited by P. Roman and H. Trice, 113–137. Philadelphia: F.A. Davis.

Krech, David, and Richard S. Crutchfield. 1948. *Theory and Problems of Social Psychology.* New York: McGraw-Hill.

Langner, Thomas, and Stanley Michael. 1963. *Life Stress and Mental Health.* Glencoe, IL: Free Press.

Lazarsfeld, Paul F. 1972. *Qualitative Analysis: Historical and Critical Essays.* Boston: Allyn and Bacon.

Lemert, Edwin. 1951. *Social Pathology.* New York: McGraw-Hill.

———. 1972. *Human Deviance, Social Problems and Social Control.* Second Edition. Englewood Cliffs, NJ: Prentice-Hall.

Lewis, Michael, and Jeanne Brooks-Gunn. 1979. *Social Cognition and the Acquisition of Self.* New York: Plenum.

Livesley, W.J., and Dennis B. Bromley. 1973. *Person Perception in Childhood and Adolescence.* London: Wiley.

Lynd, Robert S., and Helen M. Lynd. 1937. *Middletown in Transition.* New York: Harcourt Brace.

Manderscheid, Ronald. 1990. "Homelessness, Mental Illness, and Changes in Hospitalization." Paper presented at meeting of the District of Columbia Sociological Society, Dec. 6, 1990, at the American University, Washington, D.C.

Maslow, Abraham H. 1971. *The Farther Reaches of Human Nature.* New York: Viking Press.

Mead, George H. 1934. *Mind, Self and Society.* Chicago: University of Chicago Press.

Mechanic, David. 1962. "Some Factors in Identifying and Defining Mental Illness." *Mental Hygiene* 46:66–74.

Merton, Robert K. 1957. "The Role-Set: Problems in Sociological Theory." *British Journal of Sociology* 8:106–120.

———. 1976. *Sociological Ambivalence and Other Essays.* New York: Free Press.

Miller, Daniel R., and Elliot Jaques. 1988. "Identifying Madness: An Interaction Frame of Reference." In *Surveying Social Life: Papers in Honor of Herbert H. Hyman,* edited by H.J. O'Gorman, 265–286. Middletown, CT: Wesleyan University Press.

Mills, C. Wright. 1940. "Situated Actions and Vocabularies of Motives." *American Journal of Sociology* 5:904–913.

Mirowsky, John, and Catherine E. Ross. 1989. *Social Causes of Psychological Distress.* New York: Aldine de Gruyter.

Mischler, Elliot G., and Norman A. Scotch. 1970. "Sociocultural Factors in the Epidemiology of Schizophrenia." In *Social Psychology and Mental Health,* edited by H. Wechsler, L. Solomon, and B. Kramer, 128–160. New York: Holt, Rinehart and Winston.

Mischler, Elliot G., and Nancy E. Waxler. 1970. "Family Interaction Process and Schizophrenia: A Review of Current Theories." In *Social Psychology and Mental Health,* edited by H. Wechsler, L. Solomon, and B. Kramer, 235–271. New York: Holt, Rinehart and Winston.

Montemayor, Raymond, and Marvin Eisen. 1977. "The Development of Self-Conceptions from Childhood to Adolescence." *Developmental Psychology* 13:314–319.

Murphy, Jane M. 1982. "Cultural Shaping and Mental Disorders." In *Deviance and Mental Illness,* edited by W. R. Gove, 49–82. Beverly Hills, CA: Sage.

Nunnally, Jum C. 1961. *Popular Conceptions of Mental Health, Their Development and Change.* New York: Holt, Rinehart and Winston.

Parloff, Morris. 1984. "Psychotherapy Research and Its Incredible Credibility Crisis." *Clinical Psychology Review* 4:95–109.

Piaget, Jean. 1928. *Judgment and Reasoning in the Child.* London: Routledge and Kegan Paul.

———. 1932. *The Language and Thought of the Child.* Second Edition. London: Routledge and Kegan Paul.

———. 1948. *The Moral Judgment of the Child.* Glencoe, IL: Free Press.

Priest, Robert G., and Jack Steinert. 1978. *Insanity: A Study of Major Psychiatric Disorders.* London: Woburn Press.

Rabkin, Judith. 1974. "Public Attitudes Toward Mental Illness: A Review of the Literature." *Schizophrenia Bulletin* 10:9–33.

Random House. 1966. *Random House Dictionary of the English Language: The Unabridged Edition.* New York: Random House.

Reynolds, Larry T. 1990. *Interactionism: Exposition and Critique.* Second Edition. Dix Hills, NY: General Hall.

Rosenberg, Morris. 1984. "A Symbolic Interactionist View of Psychosis." *Journal of Health and Social Behavior* 25:289–302.

———. 1986a. "Self-Concept from Middle Childhood Through Adolescence." In *Psychological Perspectives on the Self*, Vol. 3, edited by J. Suls and A.G. Greenwald, 107–136. Hillsdale, NJ: Lawrence Erlbaum.

———. 1986b. *Conceiving the Self*. Malabar, FL: Krieger Publishing.

———. 1988. "Self-Objectification: Relevance for the Species and Society." *Sociological Forum* 3:548–565.

———. 1990. "Reflexivity and Emotions." *Social Psychology Quarterly* 53:3–12.

———. 1991. "Self-Processes and Emotional Experiences." In *The Self-Society Dynamic: Cognition, Emotion, and Action*, edited by J. Howard and P. Callero, 123–142. New York: Cambridge.

Rosenhan, David L. 1973. "On Being Sane in Insane Places." *Science 179:250–258.*

Rosenthal, David. 1971. *Genetics of Psychopathology*. New York: McGraw-Hill.

Rotenberg, Mordechai. 1974. "Self-Labeling: A Missing Link in the Societal Reaction Theory of Deviance." *Sociological Inquiry* 22:335–354.

Sarbin, Theodore R., and James C. Mancuso. 1980. *Schizophrenia: Medical Diagnosis or Moral Verdict?* New York: Pergamon Press.

Scheff, Thomas J. 1966. *Being Mentally Ill: A Sociological Theory*. Chicago: Aldine.

———. 1974. "The Labeling Theory of Mental Illness." *American Sociological Review* 39:444–452.

———. 1975. *Labeling Madness*. Englewood Cliffs, NJ: Prentice-Hall.

———. 1984. *Being Mentally Ill: A Sociological Theory*. Second Edition. New York: Aldine.

Schur, Edwin. 1971. *Labeling Deviant Behavior*. New York: Harper & Row.

Scott, Marvin B., and Stanford Lyman. 1968. "Accounts." *American Sociological Review* 33:446–462.

Secord, Paul F., and Barbara Peevers. 1974. "The Development and Attribution of Person Concepts." In *Understanding Other Persons*, edited by T. Mischel. Oxford: Blackwell.

Secord, Paul F., William F. Dukes, and William Bevan. 1954. "Personalities in Faces: I. An Experiment in Social Perceiving." *Genetic Psychology Monographs* 49:231–279.

Seidman, L.J. 1983. "Schizophrenia and Brain Dysfunction: An Integration of Recent Neurodiagnostic Findings." *Psychological Bulletin* 94:195–238.

Selman, Robert L. 1980. *The Growth of Interpersonal Understanding*. New York: Academic Press.

Shantz, Carolyn. 1975. "The Development of Social Cognition." In *Review of Child Development Theory and Research*, vol. 5, edited by E.M. Hetherington, 257–323. Chicago: University of Chicago Press.

Smith, Allen C., and Sherryl Kleinman. 1989. "Managing Emotions in Medical School: Students' Contacts with the Living and the Dead." *Social Psychology Quarterly* 52:56–69.

Spitzer, Robert L., Miriam Gibbon, Andrew E. Skodol, Janet B. Williams, and Michael B. First. 1989. *DSM-III-R Casebook*. Washington, DC: American Psychiatric Press.

Swann, William B. 1983. "Self-Verification: Bringing Social Reality into Harmony with the Self." In *Psychological Perspectives on the Self*, vol. 2, edited by J. Suls and A.G. Greenwald, 3–66. Hillsdale, NJ: Lawrence Erlbaum.

Szasz, Thomas S. 1961. *The Myth of Mental Illness*. New York: Hoebner-Harper.

——. 1970a. *The Manufacture of Madness*. New York: Harper & Row.

——. 1970b. "The Myth of Mental Illness." In *Social Psychology and Mental Health*, edited by H. Wechsler, L. Solomon, and B. Kramer, 35–43. New York: Holt, Rinehart and Winston.

——. 1987. *Insanity: The Idea and Its Consequences*. New York: Wiley.

Tagiuri, Renato. 1969. "Person Perception." In *The Handbook of Social Psychology*. Second Edition. Vol. 3, edited by G. Lindzey and E. Aronson, 395–449. Reading, MA: Addison-Wesley.

Thoits, Peggy. 1985. "Self-Labeling Processes in Mental Illness: The Role of Emotional Deviance." *American Journal of Sociology* 15:221–249.

——. 1989. "The Sociology of Emotions." *Annual Review of Sociology* 15: 317–342.

Vygotsky, Lev S. 1962. *Thought and Language*. Cambridge, MA: M.I.T. Press.

Weber, Max. 1949. *The Methodology of the Social Sciences*. Translated by E.A. Shils and H.A. Finch. New York: Free Press.

Weckowicz, Thaddeus. 1984. *Models of Mental Illness: Systems and Theories of Abnormal Psychology*. Springfield, IL: Charles C. Thomas.

Weiner, Bernard, I. Frieze, A. Kukla, L. Reid, S. Rist, and R. Rosenbaum. 1971. *Perceiving the Causes of Success and Failure*. Morristown, NJ: General Learning Press.

Yarrow, Marian, Charlotte G. Schwartz, Harriet S. Murphy, and Leila C. Deasy. 1955. "The Psychological Meaning of Mental Illness in the Family." *Journal of Social Issues* 11:12–24.

Index

About the Author

Morris Rosenberg received his M.A. and Ph.D. from Columbia University, and is currently professor of sociology at the University of Maryland, College Park. He has taught at Columbia, Stanford, London School of Economics, the Institute for Higher Studies (Vienna), and SUNY at Buffalo. For seventeen years he served as Chief of the Section on Social Structure, Laboratory of Socioenvironmental Studies, National Institute of Mental Health. In addition to numerous professional articles, he has published ten books, including *Society and the Adolescent Self-Image* (Wesleyan University Press, 1989), which was co-winner of the American Association for the Advancement of Science Sociopsychological Prize, and *Conceiving the Self* (Krieger Publishing Co., 1986), which received the American Sociological Association Distinguished Contribution to Scholarship Award. He teaches courses on the Sociology of the Self-Concept and the Sociology of Mental Health.